IN THE STORM

Caught in the chaos of the
Russian Revolution 1917-18

Rhoda Power (born 1890) was a children's author and broadcaster. As a young tutor in South Russia she was caught up in the terror of the 1917-18 Revolution, publishing her personal account in 1919. In 1926 with her sister Eileen, later professor at LSE, she wrote her first (of over 40) children's history books. She then pioneered her own transformational format of history radio programmes for schools, featuring dialogue sound-effects and music, becoming one of the most celebrated and widely listened-to broadcasters on the BBC. She died in 1957 but her scripts were still being used in 1970. Her book *Redcap Runs Away* (1952) is a children's classic.

IN THE STORM

Caught in the chaos of the
Russian Revolution 1917-18

RHODA POWER

Introduction by Basil Postan

Marble Hill London

Originally published in 1919 by Methuen & Co Ltd as
Under Cossack and Bolshevik

This revised edition published in 2025 by
Marble Hill Publishers
Flat 58 Macready House
75 Crawford Street
London W1H 5LP
www.marblehillpublishers.co.uk

© The Trustees of Chatham House, The Royal Institute of International Affairs 2025 © the original edition: *Under Cossack and Bolshevik* Rhoda Power
Introduction, chronology and glossary © Basil Postan 2025

All rights reserved.

No part of this book may be reproduced or transmitted in any form or by any means, electronic, mechanical, recording or otherwise, without prior written permission of the copyright owners.

A CIP catalogue record for this book is available from the British Library.

ISBN: 9781068360855
E-ISBN: 9781068360848

Typeset in Adobe Caslon
Printed and bound by IngramSpark
Text and cover design by Paul Harpin

Prefaces from the original edition

I desire to render my thanks to the Editors of "The Englishwoman" and "The Fortnightly Review," who have kindly allowed me to include in the book extracts from articles that have already appeared in print.

The names of private people in this book are fictitious

To
J.C.H.
(Eccleshall)
In whose house there is peace

When a taunt
Was taken up by scoffers in their pride,
Saying, "Behold the harvest that we reap
From popular government and equality,"
I clearly saw that neither these nor aught
Of wild belief engrafted on their names
By false philosophy, had caused the woe,
But a terrible reservoir of guilt
And ignorance filled up from age to age,
That could no longer hold its loathsome charge,
But burst and spread in deluge through the land.

Wordsworth, "*The Prelude.*"

Contents

Introduction		1
A Note on the Title		16
A Short Chronology		17
Glossary of People, Places and Parties		19
Acknowledgements		22
I.	From Newcastle to Rostov-on-Don	25
II.	A Russian Bourgeois Household	31
III.	The Revolution	44
IV.	A Criminal's Paradise	57
V.	A Journey and a Holiday	64
VI.	An Autumn of Anxiety	74
VII.	Civil War	83
VIII.	Under Cossack Protection	93
IX.	Enter the Bolsheviks	102
X.	Under Bolshevik Rule	113
XI.	The Anarchists and Departure	129
XII.	From Rostov to the Murman Coast	141
XIII.	Refugees in Murmansk	151

Illustrations and maps

Beryl, Eileen and Rhoda Power aged 4, 7 and 5	4
Rhoda: in costume, around the time of her journey to Russia	6
The Ogden's Cigarette Card, 1935	8
Rhoda Power at the BBC, as I knew her	14
Rhoda Power's railway journeys to and from Rostov-on-Don, 1916-1918	24

Introduction

IN DECEMBER 1916 a young Englishwoman in her midtwenties, unable to travel through war-torn central Europe, is about to board the steamship 'Jupiter' at Newcastle bound for Bergen in Norway. A long rail journey awaits her from there, through Sweden and Finland via Petrograd to the Southern Russian city of Rostov-on-Don on the shores of the Sea of Azov, where she has been engaged as a tutor to the teen-aged daughter of a prosperous industrialist's family. She is lighthearted, but naturally a little nervous of crossing the North Sea patrolled by German submarines. The ship makes the crossing safely, but a jolly fellow traveller's reassurance that a boat owned by a company with German shareholders would not be attacked was to prove misplaced. Within days the Bergen Steamship Line discontinues North Sea sailings after the 'Jupiter's' sister-ship 'Vega' and three others are sunk by U-boats.

The rest of her journey proves uneventful, and she is comfortably installed in the wealthy Sabarov household (not their real name; her diary suggests 'Resanov') of her 16-yearold charge. Her early account gives no hints of unexpected troubles and terrifying dangers to come. But within less than three months of her arrival she finds herself closely caught up in the early chaotic and bloody months of the Russian Revolution.

Rostov, although far from Moscow and from Petrograd, was recognised by both the 'Reds' and the 'Whites' as having crucial strategic importance in the revolutionary struggle: a major trading centre, the third largest port in European Russia handling huge volumes of grain exports, a multiple rail-head, with a number of sizeable workshops and factories, and a new university. The town was a patchwork of substantial newly-built fin-de-siècle buildings interspersed with makeshift huts and hovels but had many of the appearances of a prosperous European city. The Sabarov's large house was off Bol'shaya Sadovaya ('Great Garden Street'), its 2 ½ -mile long paved main thoroughfare, with tramlines and electric street-lighting, lined by other substantial private houses, the provincial parliament, banks, hotels, insurance companies, department stores, clubs and three cinemas.

Outwardly Rostov might have appeared conventional and established; underneath it was very unstable. The proximity of wretched urban slums and poverty alongside ostentatious affluence made it a fertile Bolshevik breeding-ground. It was also highly cosmopolitan, with a large population of Jews, Greeks and Armenians. While 'central' ethnic Russians formed the dominant ruling professional and business class they were themselves outnumbered by the 'local' Don Cossacks, who regarded themselves as strong Russian patriots but behaved as an indomitably independent-minded caste apart, adding a strong additional dose of volatility. On top of all this, the defeated 'White' military leadership had fled South from Petrograd to the Don 'Oblast' in the hope of raising a Volunteer Cossack army, while the advancing German front-line was moving ever closer from the West.

So, although distance from the centre meant that the revolutionary fuse at first burns rather slowly, the city is in fact highly combustible, as the young writer's account of the horrors she soon lives through leaves us in no doubt. She finds herself in the middle of the Battle of Rostov, the first major and bloody battle of the Revolutionary civil war and does not manage to make her perilous last-minute escape until

INTRODUCTION

the Spring of 1918 as the impending arrival of the Germans adds a further threat. Conditions become even worse after she leaves: the turmoil continues for two more years until the 'Whites' are finally driven out.

Not that she herself has an easy time after she leaves, in the midst of gunfire and slaughter. For the next three stressful months she journeys 2,000 miles from Southern Russia through Moscow, by-passing Petrograd in the grip of factional in-fighting, finally arriving on a troop train at a disease- and death-ridden make-shift transit camp at Murmansk within the Arctic Circle. She finally makes it home across the Barents and North Seas still patrolled by German submarines, in a dangerously overcrowded ship carrying 2,000 refugees but only provisioned for 800.

Her journals take the story no further; but her arrival in England does not mark the end of her travails, adding a further unspoken dimension to the narrative. On docking, the ship and its passengers are immediately condemned to be placed in quarantine. The devastating second wave of the great 'Spanish Flu' pandemic, eventually to leave 50 million dead, has been carried by troops and refugees across Northern Russia. Probably having caught it in Murmansk and already frail, she suffers from its after-effects for the rest of her life..

On her return she wrote of her experiences in magazine articles. She later expanded them into a personal memoir published as *Under Cossack and Bolshevik* by Methuen in 1919 – still topical, as violent fighting in Southern Russia around the Don continued until the summer of 1920, Rostov changing hands a further 5 times. The book certainly aroused more than passing interest at the time as it was reprinted in London and in New York. Other than in occasional academic footnotes it is now almost completely and undeservedly forgotten. Its account of the scourges of violent and murderous civil conflict,

IN THE STORM

mass movement of refugees across troubled frontiers and waters and the spread of pandemic disease speak as loudly today as they did over a century ago.

* * *

Who was this courageous young author who survived these tumultuous events and this horrific journey? What became of her on her return to England?

She was Rhoda Power, my loving gentle godmother. She was to become a pioneering and celebrated educational broadcaster and writer for children, a household name in the 1930s and '40s. Her elder sister Eileen was my father's first wife before her tragic early death. Sadly, as a small boy I knew Rhoda not well enough, and only for a short a time, before she also died too young in 1957.

Rhoda was the middle of three sisters born close together between 1889 and 1891 into a prosperous Lancashire family

Beryl, Eileen and Rhoda Power aged, 4, 7 and 5.

INTRODUCTION

which very soon traumatically fell apart. When Rhoda was only one year old, in a full-blown Victorian scandal, their stockbroker father was convicted and imprisoned for a major criminal fraud. Her abandoned mother died from tuberculosis when she was 12. Two years later their father was convicted of another fraud and received a second 5-year sentence. Her mother's spinster sisters, living in Oxford in modest circumstances, took responsibility for the girls, setting them on their way by seeing them through Oxford High School. From there all three went on to university – her two sisters to Girton College, Cambridge, Rhoda to read modern languages, political science and economic history at St Andrews University, Scotland – and then on to lead successful self-determining lives as modern single career-women.

The eldest, Eileen, became one of England's leading historians, professor at the London School of Economics, a prominent public intellectual and committed feminist. Her home in Mecklenburgh Square was a focus of internationalist left-leaning discussion and activity, and of famous parties. Pursued for her beauty as well as her brains, she resisted the advances of some of the great men-of-letters of the day until in her forties she fell in love with and eventually married my father Munia Postan, her much younger former research assistant. On her death in 1940 the great Cambridge historian GM Trevelyan wrote to him that "he knew no woman living who was her equal".

The youngest, Beryl, was an active suffragist, a senior career civil servant - during the Second World War in the Ministry of Supply helping the holiday-camp king Billy Butlin in raising the morale and productivity of munitions workers, later becoming a specialist in international labour relations, including a posting to China on secondment to the United Nations relief organization.

Rhoda did not to find it so easy as her high-performing

Rhoda: in costume, around the time of her journey to Russia

sisters to set a course for her life, after university spending some time teaching in America and doing freelance journalism. Her tumultuous visit to Russia did not mark a definitive turning-point. Back in London she still found it difficult to settle on a direction, roosting in Eileen's flat in a "little back room in

INTRODUCTION

Blooms-bur-ee", on occasions going abroad, including a stay in Palestine to work as a journalist, and continuing her travel-writing. It was not for another six or seven years, when she was in her mid-thirties, with her sister's ever-close support and encouragement, that she finally embarked on her life's work, then achieving something truly ground-breaking and remarkable of her own. She became a (perhaps the) pioneering children's educational wireless radio broadcaster.

* * *

With her sister, she published their first children's book *Boys and Girls of History* in 1926 based on which they were asked by the BBC to give six radio talks for children. Eileen had a somewhat contentious relationship with the BBC, her views apparently deemed too progressive for its mainstream establishment 'Reith-ian' culture. But Rhoda was retained as an educational broadcaster and scriptwriter, and very soon had what has been described as her 'eureka' moment from which she developed her own defining innovative idea. This was to use the full resources of the wireless to bring history vividly and immersively to life for children, by illustrating schools talks with lively passages of drama and dialogue, music and a full repertoire of sound-effects. At first these were improvised, but from 1931 were built by the BBC into a pre-recorded library.

Rhoda's unique methodology, well described as 'oral vision', became standard practice in schools broadcasting. She was acknowledged as its 'doyenne' and was herself largely responsible for its remarkable growth, which cemented her career at the BBC. It is estimated that 2,000 schools were listening at the time of her first programmes in 1927; by the outbreak of War in 1939 this number had grown to as many as 10,000. During the War the BBC scaled back its services, but not its programmes for schools. By the end of the War, during which Rhoda – now based in Bristol - estimated she wrote and narrated as many as 340 scripts, between one-third and one-half of all schools in the country were using her broadcasts.

Rhoda became the most widely-aired daytime speaker on the radio (exceeding all her male - and female - colleagues) and one of the highest-paid women professionals at the BBC. She also contributed to high-level consultations and initiatives concerning the future of educational broadcasting, including pioneering (but disregarded) advocacy of the use of television in the early 1940's. But to the surprise of many, almost certainly at her own choice, she 'undersold' herself and never moved up to more managerial roles from the creative work she excelled at and was passionate about. Her audience broadened out far beyond just schoolchildren and their teachers. She had become such a popular and well-loved household name on the radio that she was famous enough as early as in 1935 to appear on an 'Ogden's Cigarettes' card, an ultimate accolade of the day for a celebrity. Rhoda wrote drolly to a colleague: 'I keep it in my purse because it's very useful when Eileen & Beryl are given fresh academic & civic honours. I just take it out in their presence & look at it quietly & significantly, to remind them of what real fame is.'

The Ogden's Cigarette Card, 1935.

INTRODUCTION

After the War she resumed her urge to travel, venturing further afield to South, Central and North America, but continuing to write and broadcast tirelessly until her death in 1957. I cannot find a complete bibliography, but I can count over 40 listed titles. Her scripts were still being used as late as in 1970.

Her life and times until the early -1920s may have had adventitious pre-echoes of the world of today, but her life's work after then has a different and equally remarkable contemporary resonance in the post-Covid video- and online-era in which we now live: the creation of the then innovative – but now commonplace – techniques and values of remote-teaching and distance-learning.

* * *

It is tempting to give a 'trailer' to Rhoda's narrative, highlighting remarkable episodes and vivid vignettes – some comic, some frankly horrifying. Without wishing to spoil readers' satisfaction in discovering them for themselves I cannot resist spelling out some of the – to my mind – most telling.

Throughout the book she uses the words of others to illuminate her narrative. The excessive shows of affection and mindless banter in fractured English of Natasha, her spoiled and tiresome charge (whose real nick-name may have been 'Maroosa'), serve as a leitmotif to point up the disconnected insouciance and lack of understanding of her nouveau-riche social class. Reacting to the anarchic chaos after the suicide of the Don Cossack leader Kaledin, all she can say is "Pigs and gooses that they are, have taken our box in the theatre!". Later as the 'White' Volunteers allied to the Germans threaten to re-take Rostov: "All will be comfortable when the Germans make order". By contrast, the low level of political awareness of the town's 'ordinary' inhabitants is exemplified by an overheard question of one old moujik to another: " 'If we have a republic, who'll be Tsar?' 'What is a republic anyway?' asked a third. Someone hazarded, 'Perhaps it's a woman'."

When she comes to describe at first-hand the terrors of daily life from the summer of 1917 onwards, she does so with a short-hand detachment and courage that are as graphic as they are terrifying. On a brief visit to Odessa she nonchalantly records that "artillery practice appeared to take place in the garden". On her return she recounts coolly how a friend's little son is kidnapped for a ransom, tortured, starved and strangled to death. By February 1918 "Bolshevik shells are whistling over the house". One morning, having herself narrowly escaped from a gang of vengeful vigilantes out for bourgeois blood, a house servant tells her of finding the "naked body of a fair-haired boy stretched across the curb in the snow. The soldiers, who stood by it, laughed. They had sold the clothes and boots in the market and were counting the notes".

Her account of her escape by train from Rostov and Novocherkassk are perfect sound-bites, almost in the style of a contemporary radio or TV news reporter, of what has been described as the 'Railway War' being waged at the time. "We pulled up with a jerk and the sound of rifle shots suspiciously like a machine gun....Red Guards in flight before the Cossacks their cries of fright and pain unspeakably harrowing." And later, "An armoured train drew up beside us. Then a machine gun sounded and a six-inch cannon boomed....for seven hours we heard the roar of the big cannon and the maddening titter of the machine gun."

She does her best to make light of the almost unbearable conditions in Murmansk, but writes that "we lay, racked with pain and parched with fever upon our wooden planks". The children got ill and were covered with vermin and lice; some

INTRODUCTION

died. "Opposite our window men worked, nailing together the sides of wooden coffins."

Apart from Bolshevik records in Communist Party archives in Rostov on the one hand - dwelling on the misdeeds of the 'Whites' - and the published memoirs of a Tsarist cavalry officer and a young American airman attached to the RAF on the other - whose accounts are slanted against the 'Reds' – all mainly written about events after Rhoda had left, her account appears to be one of the few documented first-hand contemporary records. The historian the late Professor Brian Murphy wrote: "Neither had any regard for humane treatment of prisoners or civilians. Cruelties and atrocities abounded on all sides…To a limited extent Rhoda Power… provide(s) glimpses of how the scene may have appeared to… anti-Bolshevik observers". (Brian Murphy, *Rostov in the Russian Civil War 1917-1920*. London 2005)

My reading is that this does scant justice to her narrative. Of course, she writes from the standpoint of someone employed by, and living as a family member with, a wealthy capitalist bourgeois household; and it is true that she does not recount many specific examples of 'White' misbehaviour or any (say) of working conditions on the factory floor. But privately she admitted to having pro-Bolshevik sympathies, and throughout she shows herself – within the limits of Anglo Saxon enlightened liberal sensitivities of the time - to be even-handedly critical of the behaviour and attitudes of the bourgeoisie, alert and sympathetic to the sufferings and subservient conditions of people then customarily – but in her case not disparagingly - described as 'ordinary'. Her tone is deprecatingly light and sympathetic but detached. She vividly records increasing horrors with a dispassionate attention to detail and a sharp awareness of the confused political and social crosscurrents and their accompanying injustices and tragic outcomes. She shows her strong feelings for oppressed workers, despised Jews, abjectly poor street people and miserable conscripted foot-soldiers; all form part of her narrative. Her lack of self-pity and her delightful sense of humour and of the ridiculous are in part a cover for her courage in the face of the terrors she witnesses, and the personal danger in which she finds herself.

Under Cossack and Bolshevik shares something in common with Rhoda's later radio work for children. It is an immersive account of a passage of (albeit contemporary) history that reflects its impact on ordinary people as seen through their eyes and often in their words. It does not take much imagination to see how the book might be transcribed into a radio series of "We Were There": dramatized narrative episodes in the style of her school broadcasts, with the voices of 'ordinary' characters – her travelling companions, Natasha the infuriating teenager, street- and working- people, house-servants, old moujiks, even gangs of rough vigilantes - and the soundscape of the vivid, often horrifying, scenes she describes so tellingly.

For me this book's contemporary resonance, its literary qualities, resilient humour and its value as reportage set it apart from other accounts of the experiences of other expatriate women working or living in Russia at the same time. They may even allow comparison with such classic memoirs as *War in Val d'Orcia* by Iris Origo or *Memories* by Teffi (Nadezhda Lokhvitskaya). The latter records another journey of escape a year later than Rhoda's, but in precisely the opposite southerly direction, from Petrograd to the Black Sea.

* * *

When I first went to preparatory school in the mid-1950s we listened in our history lessons to dramatized radio broadcasts with a gentle disembodied narrator – the self-same

INTRODUCTION

Rhoda Power - and were read-to from her books. I kept to myself that she was my devoted godmother who dedicated the Puffin paperback edition of her classic children's story *Redcap Runs Away* to me – a carrot-top like her fictional hero. After my mother rendered our form teacher speechless by inviting her to tea to meet Rhoda, my star in school rose briefly to an ascendancy never to be regained.

It was not until I was much older that I began to wonder more about who she was, and how she was part of our family life. Even though I now know more, I am still struck by the twists of fate and relationships that led my Russian-born émigré father to marry his much older university supervisor and by the role played in their lives by her younger sister, of whom Eileen was solicitously protective. Rhoda had some things more closely in common with my father, her sister's lover, than Eileen did herself – as a Russian-speaker who could share the life-shaping experiences of escaping from the Revolution (his home was also in the South - not far from Odessa).

Their shock and grief when Eileen collapsed and died in Oxford Street would have brought them even closer together. But having read the book, I am less surprised that, unlike her sister, she remained single. For just once the mindless young Natasha/Maroosa was unwittingly prescient when - over 20 years earlier - Rhoda quotes her as saying,

"Oh, Little Spider dear, you will always be funny and English. So you will nevair be married."

Both women, strikingly beautiful and showing great style in how they looked and dressed, were also equally determined that nothing should deflect them from defining and following an independent path of personal and professional fulfilment unrelated to their femininity.

Only at a recent re-reading did I pay attention to the epigraph which Rhoda chose as a preface – in very small print

Rhoda Power at the BBC, as I knew her

in the original edition, but more prominent in this re-printing: Wordsworth's reflection on an earlier (French) Revolution in his autobiographical poem 'The Prelude'. It encapsulates the sentiments that inform her book's contemporary resonance. The poet attributes the woes and upheavals of his day – not dissimilar to those of our own times or to those Rhoda was writing about - not so much to what he resonantly describes as "popular governments and equality" or "false philosophy",

'But a terrific reservoir of guilt
And ignorance filled up from age to age,
That could no longer hold its loathsome charge,
But burst and spread in deluge through the land.'

INTRODUCTION

I still find it remarkable that the Rhoda I knew as a small boy in the 1950s, my frail immaculate childless late-middle-aged godmother living peacefully in Notting Hill Gate, should have been through such experiences as she describes in this book. Her passion to improve the lives and minds of countless children (myself among them) surely owed a great deal to what she learned during those years. What she did and went through over a century ago, and the manner in which she wrote about it, deserve to be better known, not least because of their relevance to the way we have to re-shape our lives today in a world defined by pandemic and violent conflict.

Basil Postan

A note on the title

THE BOOK'S ORIGINAL title *Under Cossack and Bolshevik* would have had a strong contemporary 'ring' when it was originally published, which is rather lost today. This new edition has been re-titled *In the Storm* better to reflect the events the author describes, and as a reference to the bursting 'deluge' evoked by the words of Wordsworth she used in her Preface.

IN THE STORM

A Short Chronology

December 2016-January 1917
· Rhoda Power leaves England and arrives in Rostov

February/March 1917
· Revolution breaks out in Petrograd

May 1917
· Mayday celebrations in Rostov

June 1917
· General Alexei Kaledin elected hetman of the Don Cossacks, assumes control of Rostov

October 1917
· Bolsheviks take control in Petrograd

November 1917
· General Lavr Kornilov flees Petrograd and forms 'White' Volunteer Army

26 November 1917
· Bolsheviks take control of Rostov

7 December 1917
· Kaledin regains Rostov with help of Kornilov's Volunteers; declares Don Republic

10 January 1918
· Cossack soldiers revolt against Kaledin

IN THE STORM

11 January 1918
· Kaledin loses control of Rostov; commits suicide

February 1918
· 'Whites' withdraw from Rostov.
· 'Anarchy'

23 March 1918
· Bolsheviks declare Don Soviet Republic

April 1918
· Rhoda leaves Rostov

May 1918
· 'Whites' - allied with the Germans retake Rostov

May 1918
· Rhoda arrives in Murmansk

July 1918
· Rhoda leaves Murmansk

July/August 1918
· Rhoda returns to England

GLOSSARY

Glossary of People Places and Parties

Anarchists
Tolerated by the Bolsheviks as allies against both the 'Whites' and the Mensheviks; in early 1918 they briefly filled a vacuum in the struggle against Denikin (see below) in the Don 'Oblast' and Southern Ukraine.

Ataman
A spelling of 'hetman'. A Cossack leader; refers to Kaledin (see below).

Bataisk (Bataysk)
A town some 10 miles southwest of Rostov

Brussilov
Aleksei Brussilov. Formerly a General in the Tsarist army, winning major victories against Germany; appointed by Kerensky as Commander-in-Chief in 1917 and later a key figure in the creation of the Red Army.

Cadets
Trainees at military school, prior to becoming Junker officers (see below). Also non-military 'Kadets' members of the anti-revolutionary 'KD' party.

Denikin
Anton Denikin. General in the Imperial Russian Army. Commander-in-Chief of the armed forces of South Russia during the Civil War 1917–1923.

Dobrovolchesk(i)y
Russian for 'volunteer'. Refers in general to soldiers in the Volunteer 'White' army corps recruited to fight the Germans (and later also the armed forces of the Bolsheviks); in particular to the force struggling unsuccessfully to resist the German advance from the West through Taganrog (see below).

Guluboff
Probably a reference to Golubev. An officer leading an irregular force of Cossacks from the east of the Don 'Oblast', heading for Novocherkassk and Rostov against the Bolsheviks in the Spring of 1918.

Kaledin
Aleksei Kaledin. Don Cossack Cavalry General who formed the Cossack 'White' movement in November 1917; committed suicide in February 1918.

Junkers
Young military officers in the Imperial Army. Mainly supported the 'Whites' in the Civil War.

Kerensky
Alexander Kerensky. Revolutionary leader of the Russian Provisional Government from July to October 1917 when he was overthrown by the Bolsheviks under Vladimir Lenin.

Melitz
The local civilian emergency militia.

Mensheviks
A Marxist/Social Democratic political party which supported

GLOSSARY

Kerensky (see above), losing out to Lenin and the Bolsheviks in October 1917.

Nahitchovan
A close suburb of Rostov.

Novocherkask (Novocherkassk)
Provincial capital of the Don 'Oblast' to the North-East of Rostov; the military centre of the Cossacks, but unlike Rostov not a major industrial or commercial centre. Became a haven for opponents of the Bolshevik Revolution, and hosted the headquarters of the Volunteer Army, under the command of Generals Mikhail Alakseyev and Lavr Kornilov.

Patotski
Seemingly a local 'White' military commander. Possibly Count Jerzy Pototski a pro-Czarist Polish cavalry officer.

Taganrog
An industrial city on the coast of the Sea of Azov, west of Rostov. After fierce fighting conquered by the advancing Germans in May 1918.

Tornea (Tornio)
The Finnish border town on the frontier with Sweden at the top of the Gulf of Bothnia; the rail-head for the railway line to Petrograd.

Voronej (Voronezh); Liski; Vologda; Petrozavodosk; Kandalaksha; Kola.
Passed en route on the railway journey to Moscow and then to Murmansk.

Acknowledgements

I HAVE NOT formally referenced or annotated the following sources of which I have made use, and from which I have occasionally quoted - to which I gratefully acknowledge my debt, and which readers may also find as interesting as I have.

There has been no full biography or monograph of Rhoda, although she features in the following works in which her sister Eileen is either the main or a prominent subject:

Maxine Berg's intellectual biography of Eileen Power: Maxine Berg: *A Woman in History*, Cambridge University Press, 1996

Rosemarijn van de Wal's thesis on Eileen Power's identity as a feminist historian: Rosemarijn van de Wal: *Dancing in the Kitchens of History*. Rijksuniversiteit Groningen, 2022

Francesca Wade's group biography of 5 women writers living in Mecklenburgh Square between the Wars: Francesca Wade; *Square Haunting*, Faber, 2021

Specific to Rhoda's work as a broadcaster:

10 years after her death a BBC producer discovered *Under Cossack and Bolshevik* in a BBC Library in Portland Place and wrote an admiring article in *History Today*. Stephen Usherwood: *Rostov-on-Don, 1917-1918,* History Today Volume 17 Issue 5, May 1967.

On the role of women at the BBC before the Second World War: Kate Murphy; *Behind the Wireless*, Palgrave Macmillan, 2017

ACKNOWLEDGEMENTS

Laura Carter has written a penetrating work on mid-century popular social history: Laura Carter: *Histories of Everyday Life*, Oxford University Press, 2021; and a related abstract: Laura Carter: *Rhoda Power, BBC Radio, and Mass Education*, 1922-1957, Revue Francaise de Civilisation Britannique, 2021

I greatly enjoyed reading the fascinating account by Paddy Scannell and David Cardiff; *A Social History of British Broadcasting 1922-1939*, Basil Blackwell, 1991, but was rather disappointed that Schools Broadcasting rates only three passing references. Rhoda is not mentioned; nor is her boss Mary Somerville, overall Head of Schools Broadcasting, the first woman controller of a BBC division. The index contains over 400 references to men but barely 20 to women, an indication of the change in attitudes and focus over the past 35 years!

For historical background:

The magisterial text: Orlando Figes: *A People's Tragedy*, Jonathan Cape, 1996

A real discovery, illuminating the specific background to Rhoda Power's Russian experience: Brian Murphy: *Rostov in the Russian Civil War 1917-1920*, Routledge, 2005.

Wikipedia has, as always, been invaluable.

Francis Bennett, publisher of Marble Hill, shares my childhood memories of listening to Rhoda on the BBC. He has shepherded this forgotten memoir back into print with encouragement, enthusiasm, courtesy and unrivalled expertise, for which I am profoundly grateful.

Rhoda Power's railway journeys to and from Rostov-on-Don, 1916-1918

CHAPTER I

From Newcastle to Rostov-On-Don

"WHO IS FOR RUSSIA?"

The sergeant in charge of the room walked up and down collecting passports. The little steamship "Jupiter" was to sail that night for Bergen, and the passengers, stamping their feet to warm them, waited in a building on the Norwegian wharf at Newcastle and wondered when all the formalities would finish. The air was chilly in spite of the big coal fire in one corner of the room, and the January mist penetrated the closed windows so that everything was seen through a thin grey haze. To go to Russia had, for years, been one of my dreams, and now the very atmosphere of the room, the strange, heterogeneous collection of passengers who looked so un-substantial in the mist, the vague silhouette of the ship growing out of the darkness and only distinguishable if one pressed against the window pane, had all the quality of a dream.

The cross-examination in a private office, when the military authorities asked questions almost Chestertonian in their unexpectedness, was also like part of a dream.

"Did you ever have a brother who lived at Folkestone?" said the clerk, pointing a forefinger at me.

Sunday, in *The Man Who Was Thursday*, would have answered by whispering mysteriously, "The word I fancy should be pink," or "Fly, the truth is known about your trouser-stretchers," and in a dream the reply would have been quite satisfactory, so I laughed when I thought of it, and the clerk laughed too, almost as though I had given voice to my idea, and the cross-examination proceeded in such a friendly way that I was allowed to embark within five minutes.

My berth-companion on the "Jupiter" was solid enough in appearance, but she was hardly the sort of person one would expect to be going to Russia while a European War was in progress, and so she too was one of the dream-people. She made friends with me at once.

"Goin' out to Russia, are you? Well, now, fancy that, so am I. Goin' to be married, I s'pose, aren't you? To think of 'im letting you go all that way by yourself. Downright wicked I call it." Then, in a wheedling tone, "What's 'e like, dearie; blue eyes?"

I hastily disclaimed the fictitious fiancé, and she seemed so disappointed when I said that I was going out to teach English and to learn Russian, that I felt I had not quite played the game, and did my best to entertain her till it was time to go to bed. She amazed me by undressing completely and putting on a flimsy beribboned nightgown.

"The North Sea is in the danger zone," I said.

"Now, don't you worry about submarines - we've no call to be afraid. *The Germans have shares in all these big companies* - that's a better safeguard than a life-belt." And with this comforting reflection she fell asleep.

We reached Bergen when the sun was rising and the snow-covered hills were pink-tipped, and we waited for an hour in a cold wooden shed while the customs officials examined the luggage.

Mrs. Maine, my travelling companion, shivered. "What we need is a glass of bubbly water," she said; "that'd buck us up. But come on, dearie, we must find Cooks' man and fix up about our places in the train."

Cooks' man, a merry little fellow with hair like hoar frost and twinkling blue eyes, had seen us and came hurrying towards the ticket office. He made all our arrangements, talking unceasingly in broken English, while Mrs. Maine looked at him. She had a trick of holding her muff up to her chin and peering over it with an expression of intense surprise. She did this now, and reminded me of someone playing at "Peep-bo" with a baby.

The man suggested that we should go to the hotel and rest, but Mrs. Maine shook her head.

"We'll stick to him through thick and thin," she said to me, "in case anything goes wrong. Come on, dearie, we'll do as they do in the 'alls, 'follow the man from Cooks'.'"

And it took me quite ten minutes to persuade her that it would be more interesting to explore Bergen than to remain at the ticket office from ten till four.

The time passed quickly, and when we had wandered through the town and climbed the hill so as to see the harbour from a height, we dined at the hotel and returned to the station. The train had arrived, and we took our places in the little half-coupé, where there was scarcely room to move, and at dusk we set out for Christiania. It was very cold, and all the water in the pipes froze, and every now and then the train, which could only travel slowly, stopped altogether.

Snow fell. Sometimes soft, feathery forms floated quietly and monotonously to the ground, sometimes a rushing tornado of flakes spun madly round and round like the ghosts of fallen leaves whirling in a wild dance with the wind. When the storm had cleared, I stood outside on the platform between the carriages, and we glided in and out of little towns, where the houses were painted green, red, and blue, and through forests of dark pine-trees with branches snow-laden and heavy. I watched the silver birches, slender and graceful, sway as we passed. They stood together, slim figures glimmering in the sun, like dainty brocade-clad ladies who curtsied, bending their powdered heads.

The Norwegians were friendly and kind to us, but the Swedish seemed hostile.

"Do you speak English?" we asked. They made no answer.

"Parlez-vous Français alors?" Again, we received no reply. In desperation we tried: "Sprechen sie Deutsch?"

And "Natürlich," they said crossly.

The officials at the frontier town were brusque. "Acid tablets I call then," said Mrs. Maine, as they rumpled the contents of her trunk. "If you write a book about this, you must put in *all* these details." She suddenly gurgled with laughter as a fat customs official with gold braid round his hat extracted half a bottle of whisky from her suitcase. "'Ere, young man, that's private, that is. *My!* did you ever see such a ticket? Dot 'im in your book, dearie."

It was a little difficult to obtain food on the way, and although we were supplied with bread-tickets it was not always possible to buy the bread. We got all our meals at small wayside stations, where we sat at dirty tables and took whatever happened to be before us. On these occasions there was a regular stampede across the snow, and people had no regard for one another. Mrs. Maine pushed everyone out of her way, keeping a firm hold on my wrist all the while.

"'Ere you," she said, tapping with her muff the people who incommoded her, "a little less elbow and a little more manners, if you please." It was only through her help that I managed to get a satisfactory amount to eat.

On the fourth day we reached Haparanda, the last town in Sweden, three hours late, and after a lengthy customs examination registered the luggage and drove in a sleigh to Tornea. The river was frozen so that we could drive over the route which is crossed by steamer in the summer. It was bitterly cold and the breath froze in one's nostrils. Our driver kept turning to look at us. He wore a thick, padded coat, a sheepskin hat, and boots made of some kind of skin. We passed a weary time at Tornea. After our luggage had been opened and carefully examined we were shut for five hours in a detention shed until the train arrived. One of the third-class passengers, a Russian sailor on his way home, fainted from exhaustion, and we subsequently learnt that he had had no food for two days, and had walked across the frozen river in boots which had let in the snow till his feet were blue and stiff with cold. We warmed him at the stove, and gave him hot coffee, and he prayed God to bless us and bring us good fortune.

Our journey to Petrograd was uneventful and slow. We arrived at four o'clock in the morning. The temperature was icy and there were no porters or sleighs, so that many of the passengers had to spend the night in the waiting-rooms. Fortunately I was met, and motored to an hotel, where I slept far into the next morning.

Petrograd, with its white, snow-covered streets, golden-domed churches, and gay little sleighs, was a veritable Fairyland, and I spent four days wandering round the town; sometimes going into the churches to see the pictures and mosaics, sometimes listening to the singing, which was more beautiful than any sacred music I had ever heard. I watched the long-haired priests in their vestments, bowing at the altar, swinging their censers to and fro, and occasionally stopping the service as they took little combs from their pockets to arrange their tangled locks. I passed through street after street, sitting in a sleigh behind a broad-backed coachman, who was dressed in a padded blue coat and a fur cap. I listened to the deep-toned bells of St. Isaac's, and saw the Winter Palace gleaming in its setting of snow.

IN THE STORM

It was with regret that I tore myself away from this wonderful city. But tickets for the south-going trains were sometimes difficult to get, because many people were leaving the capital owing to the food problem, and they booked their places in advance, so that I had to seize whatever opportunity presented itself. It took three days to reach Rostov, and I spent most of the time looking out of the window at the wide spaces and tracks of forest-land, and wondering whether the Sabaroffs, with whom I was going to live, would prove agreeable companions. There were only three people in the carriage beside myself, but it was airless, as the double glass windows would not open, and I was glad when the train pulled up, though the station was half under water and the waiting-room, crowded with dirty peasants, smelt of stale sausage.

CHAPTER II
A Russian Bourgeois Household

ROSTOV-ON-THE-DON cannot be described as a typical Russian town, though possibly it is quite a good example of a South Russian trading centre. When I had been there for some weeks I realized that there were more Greeks, Armenians, and Southern Jews than Russians and Cossacks, and that society was divided into numberless cliques. The Jews, many of whom were said to have become rich since the outbreak of the European War, were admitted into society, but were considered "outsiders," and invited to few of the big social functions. This, however, hardly affected them, as they were sufficiently numerous to organize their own entertainments.

For an Englishwoman, accustomed to freedom of opinion and toleration regarding religious sects, the attitude of the Russian bourgeoisie and peasantry towards the Jews was amazing. The peasants quite frankly hated them and made no bones about it. If one mentioned a Jew by name they used to spit on the ground. The better educated classes also despised them, and though they invited the good families to dinner on rare occasions, they seldom had their own friends to meet them.

"Who played tennis with you to-day?" I once asked my pupil.

"Oh, Peter Petrovitch, Marie Vassilovna, and a Jew." He was not worth mentioning by name.

The Greeks for the most part had lived in the town for

many years and had become quite Russianized, some of them being unable to speak their mother tongue. Others, however, still preserved Greek customs, had their own native servants, and ate the usual Greek dishes when they could procure the proper ingredients. One family, consisting of nine girls, the eldest of whom was twenty-six and the youngest six, were brought up with the old Greek idea of the dependence of women, and could never leave the house without first obtaining permission from their father, who required to know exactly where they were going and when they would return. If both father and mother were out they were obliged to remain at home until their parents returned.

The élite of Rostov society lived in big houses off the main street, which was flanked on either side by fashionable shops and led to the public garden. Their rooms always struck me as being intensely uncomfortable and formal in appearance. One missed the friendly hearth of the English houses. The petch (stove), tiled and forming a portion of the wall, gave plenty of heat but was cheerless. The atmosphere, too, was unpleasantly hot, as in the winter the double-paned windows were tightly closed and every crack sealed with paper so that the cold air could not penetrate.

Each room had its icon placed high up in the corner near the ceiling, and whenever an orthodox family migrated to a new house the priest was invited to bless the rooms, after which there was much feasting. The wedding icon, given to the owners of the house on their marriage, hung in their bedroom, and was usually exquisitely decorated with pearls. The richer the family the more beautiful was the icon. A little lamp burnt before it night and day, and was only extinguished for the purpose of replacing the wick.

I was a foreigner, so there was no icon in my room, but the old nurse took my little Medici print of St. Francis preaching to the birds and hung it at the head of my bed. She called it "the stranger's religion" and crossed herself whenever she dusted it. I loved this sweet, withered old woman, who suffered so much and so patiently. She was almost blind and crippled with rheumatism, due, she told me, to having been obliged to sleep on the floor outside a nervous mistress's door.

She wondered at my indignation and explained carefully, "But she was my mistress, barishnia, and unless I was there she was afraid to sleep."

She took a strange fancy to me and mothered me when I was ill, but sometimes her ministrations were prejudicial to my recovery. I shall never forget the day I was suffering from sickness and she brought me a flabby pancake followed by a plate of thin soup, floating in which was a fish's head with bulging white eyes. When the family was at the theatre she used to wander into my room and talk by the hour, telling me of her life in the Cossack village, and how, when she was fifteen, her mother-in-law had proved such a hard task-mistress that she had tried to drown herself in the well.

She always wanted to know what we had to eat, and when I told her she threw up her hands in horror, exclaiming, "Ei, ei! What would become of me there? You must not go back, my little one."

She was amazed when I told her how much I disliked dining at three in the afternoon after lunching at one. Her pride in living in a place like Rostov, where there were so many large houses, was rather pathetic. She called it "our town."

The appearance of "our town" was curious, and gave one the same impression as a picture by a cubist. It seemed to be all higgledy-piggledy, a jumble of vivid colours, domes, and oddly shaped houses. Next to a large and ornate mansion with statues at the door and twisted iron gates there was a tiny wooden hut thatched with straw and built half underground, so that the windows were on a level with the road. The first was the property of some wealthy merchant who had his garage and stables, and possibly a garden, while the quaint little hut at its side belonged to a poor workman who had collected a few sticks of furniture for himself and his family, and refused to be bought up. The interior of these cottages was unspeakably dirty, and the smell of humanity and stale food overwhelming. Children, poultry, and dogs crawled about the floor indiscriminately, and there was always very little light. Coloured oleographs of the Tsar and other prints were nailed to the walls, and every cottage had its holy pictures and icon. The bed, when there was one, seemed to be an object of care, and the blanket was almost invariably neatly folded and the pillow hidden by a cover richly embroidered in red and blue cross-stitch. The samovar had a place of state in the corner, and there was generally a big flat stove on which the chilly old folk used to sleep.

The shops, too, had much the same effect as the houses. Big, fashionable bazaars stood next to tiny stores built a little way back from the pavement and floored with stones between which earth and grass peeped. These little insigificant places were often owned by quite rich Greek fruiterers, and sometimes one could buy from them what the larger and more fashionable shops could not supply. Outside each shop there was a coloured wooden board on which various goods for sale within were painted, execrably out of drawing and crude, but useful to the bewildered foreigner, who could lead the salesman outside and point to the object she desired, uttering without more ado the simple word "dyti" (give).

Shopping in Russia could be very complicated when one did not know the language. Words with totally different meanings, but very much alike in form, were always leading one astray. For instance, I strode confidently into a shop, and asked the astonished man for a "little thief" (voreshka). I explained haltingly that I required it for parcels, and it was only after I had exercised my pantomimic powers to the utmost that he guffawed loudly, and gave me a piece of string (verovka).

There were three markets in Rostov, where one could buy anything from wooden toys to house-linen, and it was amusing to do one's shopping there in the early morning when the poor people were driving hard bargains. The peasants, wrapped in thick coats or leather shoobas lined with sheepskin, stood behind their booths under wooden shelters, stamping their feet on boards thrown down to protect them from the snow, and chattering like rooks. "Come, barishnia. These apples are the best, and cheap, but the cheapest in Russia."

"No, no, little aunt, these are all spotted with blight."

"Tfuh!" (spitting). "The bourguika does not know what is good" - and her neighbour, "Come to me, take my apples, dear."

"Now, look here, those are polished on this side and bruised at the back."

"Bruised! Bojé moy! the little dove does not know the colour of an apple."

And so on until one was eventually obliged to take a very inferior article at an exorbitant price, for which one had bargained for about ten minutes. The second-hand clothing store was patronized more than other booths, and I am quite sure that if some rich mistress were to have risen early and gone to the market she would have found many a silk petticoat and crêpe de Chine blouse which she had long missed from her cupboard, for the servants were badly paid and took advantage of unlocked drawers.

I was very sorry for the servants: they led such uncomfortable lives; and though they nearly all seemed to be thieves and liars I could not help liking them. They spoke in such musical sing-song voices, used such quaint phraseology, and were so easily amused and haphazard, and had such an unshakable belief in the gadalka (fortune-teller), whom they consulted whenever they were in love or had lost something.

They were not particularly well treated, unless they happened to be living with cultured people, and many of them had no bedrooms, but slept rolled up in shawls on the kitchen table or sometimes on the floor. They were not supplied with bedding, as it was generally supposed they would sell anything of which they had the use.

They rarely undressed, and slept in their everyday clothes, and sometimes in the long felt top boots which they wore in the streets. Many of them went about their tasks barefooted because shoes were expensive, and they did not earn enough to buy new ones. They were rarely clean and always untidy. Uniform seemed only to be worn by parlourmaids, who were seen by visitors and so had to look neat. The cook was called by her fellow-servants "Little Mother," the laundress "Aunt," and the old nurse, "Grandmother"; and they cuffed the young housemaids and screamed at them till I sometimes thought their lives must be hardly worth living.

There was a general understanding among them that the younger ones should help their elders to cheat the master and mistress, and should say nothing when the laundress used the household soap for washing her friends' linen (at a fixed price), provided she occasionally ironed a blouse or two for the girls. The cook thought nothing of telling her mistress that food was double its actual price, and pocketing the extra money given her to pay the market women. She kept the younger servants' tongues quiet by stealing sugar for them and sometimes baking them cakes. On the whole, they were fed pretty well, though it was difficult to procure a variety. The parlourmaids came off best, and sometimes if one opened the dining-room door suddenly one would find them outside with their mouths full, or dipping their fingers into dishes, to taste what was going to be set before the family.

Hardly a servant in the town could read or write, and they spent their spare time playing cards or sewing a little, but often sitting with their hands in their laps doing nothing at all. We had a charming little housemaid, twenty-one years of age, with a rosy, laughing face, and roguish brown eyes. She was rather more intelligent than the others, and had bought a child's copy-book, and, after dinner used to sit in the greenhouse, her tongue between her teeth, her fist crumpled like a baby's, laboriously copying up-strokes and down-strokes. I doubt, however, if she knew what the hieroglyphics represented.

She was married and had a child of four, but as her husband was at the Front she had drifted into domestic service, leaving the child with her mother-in-law. Her name was Aniuta, and because she was married she imagined that she was wiser than the other servants, and could do things better. She called them scornfully "those girls," and she was the youngest of all.

"I, I have been married five years. I know the world. Those girls, how can one expect them to work well; they know nothing. Pah! they are more ignorant than the dogs in the yard."

And with a toss of her brown head and a swirl of her red cotton skirt she would return to her copy-book. She left us after a few weeks with a little cardboard box in one hand and her wages in the other. Her husband had come back from the Front, followed her from her native village to Rostov, presented her with a railway ticket, and ordered her to return with him. Anita was overwhelmed.

"But think, barishnia, I know him not. I know not his ways, his habits. I am not used to him, and now has he not a beard? But it is impossible." And she refused to go.

IN THE STORM

I heard afterwards that he took her by the ear and asked her how many "cavaliers" she had at Rostov, and she, hunching her shoulder because of the pain, said she would rather flirt with ten cavaliers than live with one animal. Nevertheless, she went away with the animal, and "those girls" laughed at her from the kitchen window.

The men-servants were picturesque creatures and delightful liars.

The explanations they offered for the disappearance of articles which they had undoubtedly stolen caused me to have the liveliest respect for their ingenuity. The storoj, who guarded the house at night, and the dvornik, who swept out the yard and did odd jobs, were great friends. They had a code of knocks on the wall by which they used to wake one another, and when the rest of the household slept.

Dmetri, the dvornik, used to creep to the garden gate with anything he happened to have pilfered, and pass it through the bars to the storoj, who sold it to some of his cronies waiting in the road, and shared the booty with Dmetri. Of course they drank, not vodka, for it was difficult to get, but a sort of alcoholic furniture polish which had the same effect. This drinking was not exactly regular, but systematic; that is to say, they would be perfectly sober for months on end, and then suddenly have a bout for three weeks, after which they would wake up one morning with splitting headaches and find they had no money left. They took it very philosophically. What were the wages for? On these occasions they were generally maudlin and apologetic.

"You'll forgive me, barinia, won't you?"

"Certainly I will forgive you, but you must not do it again."

"What, does the barinia mean I mustn't go on till the end of the month?"

The storoj had an understanding with the coachman

that at midnight, if his employers were in bed, he should be let into the stables where a rug would be ready for him and where he could sleep till breakfast-time, when he would once more return to the front door, and sit with the virtuous air of one who had been there all night, ready to greet the master when he left the house. I discovered his shortcomings quite by accident on a winter evening, when he ought to have been at the door to let me in after a party, and I spent the best part of an hour shivering in the snow and trying to make him hear. He met me with a most disarming smile, expressed a hope that I had spent a pleasant evening, and held out his hand for the expected tip. The family slept peacefully every night thinking they were well guarded, so I suppose the old villain unintentionally served his purpose.

Natasha, my pupil, treated them all with the greatest contempt. "They are real pigs," she used to say in her broken English; "what good to be polite with them when they steal all time and are dirty?"

I suggested that if they were treated with greater respect they would improve, but she laughed and said they were used to it. Certainly she had no consideration for them, and they waited upon her hand and foot, rushing to answer her imperious peal at the bell, and arriving out of breath for fear of bringing upon their heads a tirade against slowness.

Nearly all the young girls of the nouveau riche bourgeois class so predominant in Rostov had the same attitude towards the servants. They were paid to work, and so they were given very little peace. They had to do the barishnia's hair, lace her boots, dress her, and even bathe her. This bathing was almost like a sacred rite, and was undertaken with the greatest solemnity. As there was no central boiler, the water had to be specially heated, and this took a long time. Wood was scarce, and so the bath was only used once a week.

At first I found this a great deprivation, but afterwards, when I had secured a daily substitute in the shape of huge cans of boiling water from the kitchen (thereby earning for myself the title of "Mees Gariachia Vada"-"Miss Hot Water"), I was rather relieved, as bath-night always seemed the occasion of a general upset. The servants, in white overalls rolled up at the elbow, and white handkerchiefs round their heads, their faces scarlet with the exertion of scrubbing, were usually in tears. An irate damsel in the bath was shouting orders at the top of her voice, water was splashed all over the floor, and the passage was full of smoke from the wood fire.

The housemaid was very much troubled when I refused to admit her while I was having a bath. Her idea was that I could not possibly reach my back. As I never once allowed her to come in she is now firmly convinced that the English are a very dirty race. The master of the house was bathed by a white-coated valet, and on those days he arrived at the tea-table actually waxed and perfumed. I never could get accustomed to this, nor to meeting him at breakfast in his green plush dressing-gown and felt slippers.

My pupil's education was typical of that given to the Russian bourgeois who was not sent away from home. Many girls went to "institutes" or boarding schools, where they had much less liberty than the day-girls at the "gymnasiums" (high schools). They wore, as a rule, old-fashioned and ugly uniforms with broad collars and aprons. They were seldom allowed outside the school grounds, and had to conform to all sorts of irksome rules regarding the way they did their hair, etc.

Natasha attended the gymnasium daily and passed her public examination there. She had both German and an English governess, and a French lady came to the house once a day to talk French with her, so that she was thoroughly conversant with all three languages. Visiting masters and mistresses gave her extra coaching in the school subjects in which she was not proficient. A ballerina taught her dancing, and she had music lessons from a master who lived in the town. She received all her teachers in her bedroom, as the dining-room was sacred to meals and the drawing-room to guests.

Natasha herself took very little interest in anything she had to learn, and made no attempt to master what was difficult. She detested writing essays, and so paid a teacher five roubles to do this for her. There seemed to be very little honour among teachers and pupils. I was told that the rich girls who had written a bad exercise sometimes slipped a ten rouble note into the leaves of their books and eventually received full marks. At the viva voce lessons many of them attached a paper with the correct answers written on it to an elastic sewn into their sleeves. From this they read the lesson, and when accused of holding a paper they let go the elastic, which slipped up their sleeves, and showed empty hands. Even parents were known to bribe the masters, and girls who did not know their lessons often paid cleverer pupils to write their answers.

Rostov, after the fall of Warsaw, became a university town, and advertisements sometimes appeared in the local paper to the effect that students would write gymnasists' essays at the rate of a rouble per hundred words, or two roubles if full marks were expected. Nobody seemed to think anything of this, and the students in question quite fearlessly published their names and addresses. Many of these young men were so poor that they would do anything to earn a little money. I remember a particularly attractive quartet who shared an attic in one of the houses in a back street. They could only afford one meal a day, and used to wander arm in arm through the town, flirting over their shoulders with all the prettiest girls, and singing with their starved voices. It was tacitly understood that they were never invited out to dinner together as they had only one good pair of shoes between them.

Her last day at school was a great event in a Russian girl's life. She received her certificate and was considered a "young lady" The occasion was celebrated in various ways, but there was always a party to which the young friends were invited. The parents gave their daughter handsome presents, the rooms were filled with flowers, and there was sometimes dancing. Natasha was delighted when she left the gymnasium, as she could discard her uniform and attend those cinemas from which schoolgirls were excluded, the pictures shown at these institutions being divided into two classes - those to which a young girl might go, and others suitable for an older person. Of course the schoolgirls evaded the law.

The close of her scholastic career marked the beginning of a life of leisure for Natasha, as was the case with most young girls who did not continue their studies at the university. She literally had no interests beyond the theatre and the cinemas. She had so much money that everything she should have done for herself was done for her, and she sometimes cried for sheer boredom.

"Que voulez-vous?" said her governess to me, "maintenant elle attend le mari."

And it was true. "How I wish I could marry me," she used to say, flinging her arms above her head and gazing into space, "I would not mind even if I did not love so I could marry now at the once. I am already seventeen, and did not grandmother marry when she was fourteen?"

"But, Natasha, if you married some one you did not care for, later you might meet some one you loved, and then your life would be ruined."

"Pooh! I would take a lovair. It is easier so if there are children."

It was useless to expostulate. I could only point out the disadvantage of such an arrangement. She used to listen with her eyes half closed and her head on one side, and then suddenly throw her arms round my neck, saying between kisses. "Oh, Little Spider", (her name for me because I was thin), "dear, you will always be funny and English. So will you nevair be married." We usually left it at that.

CHAPTER III
The Revolution

WE LED A slack, luxurious life for the first month after my arrival, driving in the sleigh or the car, going to theatres or cinemas nightly, and eating the rarest dainties. In our house white bread, milk, and sugar were plentiful. We had cakes every day. How this was possible I do not know, seeing that we had tickets for a limited allowance of sugar and flour. There were, however, sacks of each hidden in an unused room. A certain amount was given out daily to the cook, and when the contents of the sacks began to get low they were replenished. And while we ate cakes and chocolates at twenty roubles a pound, caviare, and good fresh meat, peasants stood shivering hour after hour outside the bakery, their tickets clutched between blue fingers, waiting for a loaf of bread.

If there were not enough to go round they went away empty handed. Some of them lined up at midnight and waited till the shops opened in the morning. They had families to feed and could not be turned away. I used to watch their patient, tired faces, and the pale little children, sitting in the snow on overturned baskets, and wonder how long it would be before they would rebel. A little white-faced factory-girl haunted my dreams. It was Anna Ivanova, an orphan with two small brothers. She used to stand at the bakery door, her head wrapped in an old brown shawl, her thin body shivering with cold as the snow beat relentlessly against her. She always carried a large basket and waited, one of many, in the long queue outside the shop, her eyes looking straight in front of her, her chin thrust slightly forward, the picture of utter weariness.

Many other women stood before her and many behind, all with a look of dogged patience on their faces. Only when the door opened to admit the first five did a momentary gleam of interest creep into their eyes.

Day after day Anna stood at this door, sometimes in the middle of the line of women, sometimes at the end. Her position depended upon the time it took her to walk from the factory where she worked, and though she tried to move quickly she had often to stop and rest because her limbs, weary with standing, refused to support her. Long hours at the factory, where she earned a mere pittance, the time she spent outside the bakery waiting to change her bread ticket for a loaf, and the haunting anxiety lest there should not be enough bread to go round, began to tell.

Anna Ivanovna grew paler and more fragile every day. As time went on she seldom managed to take her place among those at the beginning or in the middle of the line, but stood among the later ones, and after a dreary waiting was often sent away empty handed, for the scarcity of food increased daily. At last there came a day when she was later than usual. Those among whom she used to stand looked for her anxiously, and when she did not appear some shrugged their shoulders, but others gazed across the steppes and wondered. . . . Anna Ivanovna was dead.

They wrapped her in the old brown shawl, and two men in white cowls carried the poor emaciated body in an open coffin. The thin face was uncovered so that all who cared to look might see Anna Ivanovna in her last sleep. A priest walked in front with a banner, and two white clad figures, carrying the black coffin lid, followed him. Anna's little brothers, carefully holding a picture of the Virgin and Child, wrapped in an embroidered towel, came behind. There was no sound but the "crunch, crunch" of the snow as it powdered under their feet, and the hoarse cries of a few blackbirds flying low in front of the coffin, As the little procession passed the bakery where Anna had spent so many weary hours, the women crossed themselves, and one whispered to another: "Yesterday Michael Grigorovitch, to-day Anna Ivanovna, to-morrow perhaps thou, perhaps I. Who knows? It is the price of war."

Many things were the price of war, but they were only apparent in the streets and by-ways, and certainly not in our house. We lived on the fat of the land. The war scarcely seemed to touch us. Life consisted in seeking amusement - always amusement - to pass the time. There were days which seemed almost too long, and one yearned for the rush of an English war-time week, with hardly time to get through the work. Visits were paid to the hospitals, and cigarettes and fruit given to soldiers, but in many cases these too seemed only a pastime, and when the scarcity of food increased were abandoned.

When we were driving in the town we often met detachments of soldiers on their way to the station. They always sang a curious melancholy chant, now all together, now in solo. They, too, were the "price of war." I did not realise, until I was told, that they were off to the Front; they seemed so inadequately prepared. Their boots were bad, and where they gaped at the back were stuffed with bits of old sacking. Sometimes there was one rifle between three men.

"I suppose they will be armed when they get to the fighting line," I said.

"Perhaps. But I don't think so. You see, there are a great many of them and there is not enough equipment."

"But surely the Government knows. It is abominable. We ought to organize a protest."

"It is a good thing you are talking English; otherwise you would get us all into trouble. Do be careful."

Every time I met these soldiers I thought that it would

THE REVOLUTION

not be possible for them to stand such conditions for long, and that Russia would be obliged to give in. Everything indicated that a change, and a sudden change, must take place. The country was literally worn-out. An influx of refugees had helped to cripple her resources, food was scarce, the prices of necessities rising daily, the soldiers badly equipped and their families hungry. But the people seemed so patient and resigned, so filled with a sort of melancholy fatalism, that it was obvious only something sudden and brilliant would rouse them.

And then the Revolution came.

We in the south could not realize what was happening. We felt rather than knew that something had changed, that the old life was passing away and that somewhere a struggle was taking place. News from Petrograd ceased suddenly. For days the newspapers did not arrive, and only local trains shunted into the station. Groups of people stood at the street corners gossiping, stopping the passers-by.

"Have you had any news?"

"None, have you? There's something in the air."

The wildest rumours were current, and food riots were threatened; the streets were crowded, and nobody seemed to go to bed. Three days passed. The tension increased, and just when it seemed as though the people could wait no longer a messenger came from the station, and in less than half an hour the whole town knew that the Tsar had abdicated, and that the students and workmen were fighting against the police in the streets of Petrograd.

Riots were feared in Rostov, and many of the rich people expected pogroms, but the town was wonderfully orderly, and but for the open-air meetings, the processions, and red flags of liberty floating everywhere it might have been an ordinary feast-day.

Definite news from Petrograd did not come in for several

IN THE STORM

days, and of course rumours increased. We heard that the Tsarina had been murdered and that all the royal palaces were in flames. Later this was denied, and when the actual news began to arrive the rejoicing was so great that many of the rich merchants, stricken with panic, doubled the guard round their houses and closed their shops; but there were no excesses, and the contrast to the situation in Petrograd was very marked. The following letter received from a friend living in Petrograd at the time shows how differently the two towns were affected:

"On Friday, March 9th, over the Petrogradsky side there had been much rioting, trams overturned, and shops pillaged, etc. Here, the streets were crowded with work-people on strike, all apparently very pleased with themselves. Suddenly a huge crowd came surging along, pursued by mounted Cossacks. I watched them pass. What struck me most was that the Cossacks, who are usually selected to do the dirty work of Russia, were singularly gentle with the mob, which was not in the least afraid of them. On Saturday the temper of the people began to be very nasty, and on Sunday there was a real massacre.

"It appears that five thousand machine guns had been put on the roofs of the principal buildings, ostensibly for the purpose of defending the city against the Germans, but, as one is reluctantly obliged to admit now, in anticipation of the revolution. The police began firing on the people. The different regiments gradually went over to the people after firing one against the other. Officers were shot or bayoneted, and of course many old grudges were avenged. I saw from the window three motor-lorries full of dead bodies flung in anyhow, and then a very young officer, who refused to give up his sword, shot dead, and lastly, which drove me away once and for all from that window, a policeman bayoneted, and then his face jumped on by six soldiers....

"In the evening the soldiers came to take away old

THE REVOLUTION

General K- -, who lived in the flat below ours. He is well over eighty. The servants rushed out to see, and the cook, a woman of about forty, stood screaming after him, 'Hurrah, old devil, you will soon be red meat!' He was released the same night, but died from the shock.

"At ten p.m. things were at their worst. Have you ever heard a mob howl? Well, I pray God you never may. Mingled with the howling there were the screams of people being done to death. The streets were red, red, red. The next morning the shooting continued. Officers were being disarmed, and, if they offered any resistance, shot. At a quarter to four that afternoon our house was attacked and the soldiers came swarming up, swearing some one had been shooting from the window. I denied this, but they set the machine guns on us and blazed away for over an hour....

"My sympathies are entirely with the people. They have been abominably treated. The city was full of flour and sugar when it was searched. ..."

After a few days the excitement in Rostov died down, to the disgust of the newsboys, who tried to accelerate their sales by shouting that the Kaiser had committed suicide, and that the Crown Prince had hanged himself. The people began to organize meetings in order to ascertain their position under the new regime. The police, like the Snark-hunter, "softly and silently vanished away." In any case they had no power, for they were deprived of their fire-arms, and the people simply refused to recognize them. Meetings, which had hitherto been considered criminal offences, were held in the town gardens, in the streets in fact, everywhere.

There was much cheap oratory and a few earnest, soul-stirring speeches, and the students spent their time in showing how the new democracy would affect the lives of the Russian people. It was curious to watch these young men, standing on broken chairs or on the railings, their eyes burning with enthusiasm, enumerating one by one the points in favour of the new regime, and gently trying to explain, as though they were teaching children, how the peasants would benefit. Young workmen listened, doggedly silent and incredulous, or wildly enthusiastic; girls with bright handkerchiefs round their heads stood open-mouthed, drinking in every word; old bearded moujiks nudged each other, but did they understand?

"That's good," said one; "the boy's right, and he has learning."

"But," objected another, "if we have a republic, who'll be Tsar?"

"What is a republic, anyway?" asked a third.

Some one hazarded, "Perhaps it's a woman."

"Well, perhaps she's good-looking. Hurrah, tovarishchi (comrades)! hurrah for the republic"—and away they went, thoroughly pleased, leaving the speaker still on the chair, helplessly staring at their vanishing backs and wondering whether he himself was quite certain as to the meaning of democracy.

If the average peasant did not understand the terms "republic" and "democracy," he certainly thought he realized the full significance of the word "liberty." He was just like a child whose nurse was on a holiday; he was at a loose end and thought he could do whatever he pleased. Men and women in domestic service had attended a large meeting and had passed a resolution that they would no longer be called "thou" by their employers, and that they would not work more than eight hours a day; so that a servant, if she had risen in the morning at seven, would often refuse to do any work after three o'clock in the afternoon, regardless of the fact that she had probably spent several hours sitting in the kitchen doing nothing. Any remonstrance brought the stereotyped reply: "Now it is liberty."

In our household this meeting produced a wild disorder. The maidservants celebrated it by giving a party. Only the old nurse wept unrestrainedly in a corner for her Tsar. "Ei, ei! the little father has gone. What will become of us all?"

Neither the coachman nor the chauffeur had been required during the day, and had been ordered to be ready at 7.30 p.m. to take the family to the theatre. Seven-thirty chimed but no conveyance arrived. Eight o'clock struck and a furious master sent for the housemaid. What had happened to cause this inconvenient delay?

"Cvoboda" (liberty).

The dvornik was ordered to harness the horse and to drive the barin and barinia to the theatre. But the car and the carriage, not to mention the horse, were missing.

"Cvoboda," repeated the maid stolidly. And, indeed, as it was after three o'clock, the car and the carriage were helping to celebrate the liberty of the people and were taking the chauffeur's friends for joy-rides in the town. The barishnia wept and wished the Cossacks would come and force the "simple people" to work; but the Cossacks shared the respect for Cvoboda and so nothing could be done. Of course the chauffeur was dismissed. He grinned, and hinted that very soon the "bourgzhui" (bourgeoisie) would not require chauffeurs as they would have no cars, and sure enough, shortly afterwards, all motor cars were commandeered by the Soldiers' and Workers' Union, though ours remained in the garage as it was too weak for their work.

Engaging a new man to take the place of the one, who had been dismissed, was a difficulty. Every one, who applied for the post required such a large salary and so much free time that it seemed hardly worth while keeping a car. An amusing dialogue through the telephone was afterwards reported to me, and it showed how the attitude towards the "intelligentsia" was gradually changing.

Illiterate Voice: "Is Sabaroff in?"

Mme. Sabarova (stiffly) : "Gospodin (Mister) Sabaroff is not at home."

Illiterate Voice (loftily): "Oh, well, when Sabaroff comes back tell him to ring up Gospodin Chauffeur."

Home life, and in many cases labour, became completely disorganized. In households where a sense of humour lurked, the phrase, "Now it is liberty," became a standing joke, and the members of the family just shrugged their shoulders and did the work themselves. Servants, who wished to go to the cinema, sauntered out of the house when they pleased; workmen, bored with what they were doing, temporarily downed tools and strolled off to meet their friends or organized meetings during working hours to discuss any grievance that was rife. The streets were disorderly. There was no bloodshed, but meetings were held everywhere, so that it was impossible to walk, and one was continually being pushed off the pavement by people who were hurrying to join the crowds listening to a favourite speaker. The Jews were much more conspicuous than they had been before, and, at the time, this was not generally resented, though when the new government gave them the rights of citizenship the move was adversely criticized, particularly among the illiterate inhabitants of the town.

An amusing occurrence took place at one of the big general meetings of the peasants when an old Jewess got up to speak and was howled down.

"But now we are sisters," she pleaded.

"How is that possible," said a raucous voice from the background, "when you haven't been baptized?"

The meeting broke up in confusion.

During this time discipline among the soldiers gradually

weakened. Spring had set in, and those who had not yet given up wearing their sheepskins must have suffered acutely. The convalescent men in the hospitals, who had hitherto been obliged to remain in the gardens and to dress respectably, discarded most of their clothing and wandered through the streets, barelegged, wearing a sort of white pyjamas. They used to sit about the pavements and on the steps outside the shops, and the members of the public were shocked. Officers were never saluted and were openly mocked.

I, myself, saw a party of soldiers go up to two captains seated at a table in a restaurant and blow cigarette smoke into their faces.

Peace talk was heard everywhere, especially among the peasants, who, though they were still enthusiastically on the side of the Allies, understood sooner than most people that Russia was too worn out to continue fighting. The bad news from the Front and the desertions from the army enhanced this idea, and we began to realize that though the Cossacks might struggle to the bitter end, the ordinary Russian soldiers would gradually lose their faith and drift back to their quiet home life. They were tired of the war and said so frankly, and at the pacifist meetings hardly a dissentient voice was heard. In any case, they asked, what good was the war doing them? They only wanted to be quiet and enjoy their new liberty, and how could they do this if they had to fight? What was the war *for*? The question always remained unanswered, and the crowds dispersed talking eagerly of peace.

The May Day procession, so picturesque and so wonderfully organized, showed better than anything else the temper of the people at the moment. The weather was perfect, and not a cloud was visible. The sky was brilliantly blue and the sun shone. The snow had long since melted, so that the trees were in bud and the air full of promise. No better day could have been chosen to celebrate the triumph of liberty. Strains of the "Marseillaise" and the tramp of many feet heralded the procession, and at eight o'clock we went to the windows and saw, coming towards us, hundreds of men, women, and children, wearing the scarlet revolutionary caps, and marching under banners printed with the words: "Hail to Democracy," "Long life to the Russian Republic," "We have won Liberty, now we want Peace," "Land for the People," etc.

When they passed our house they burst triumphantly into song, throwing back their heads as they sang, some with the tears in their eyes, others with a smile on their lips. On and on the procession came, the voices swelling in volume. It was a remarkable sight.

"God!" whispered a young officer in mufti, behind me, "where shall we be next year?"

And still the singing continued, now wild and sad, now triumphant and joyous, and yet beneath it all there was that curious undercurrent of melancholy resignation. The heartbeats of Russia are felt more potently in her music than in anything else. First a troop of women passed, red-clad, walking under an arch of banners, greeting a democracy that had recognized the justice of their claim to citizenship; after them, a vast horde of peasants and work-people demanding an eight-hour day; then the students, future doctors, lawyers, teachers, all types; the starved workers who had paid for their books by going without meals; the dreamers with eyes full of vision; the out-at-elbow young optimist jogging along with "There's a good time coming" written all over his beaming countenance; the pessimist walking apologetically and whispering to his neighbour that one could be sure of nothing in this life; the young sportsman, quick to pick up a new dance, and slow at his studies, not quite knowing what it was all about, but wanting "to be in the thing, you know?" I picked them out

THE REVOLUTION

and laughed and sang with them, and wanted to rush out and shake them by the hand, and do mad things.

And still they came, a vast, un-receding wave. After the students walked the schoolgirls in brown dresses and neat black aprons, singing in sweet, clear voices, some of them quaintly serious, others giggling, with linked arms, and making little moues over their shoulders at the boys who came behind them; then a band of little girls under a banner, showing that even the women of the future realized they had entered their kingdom. Then, again, hundreds of factory-girls, some pathetically young and delicate, whose white faces contrasted horribly with their scarlet caps of liberty. They, too, carried banners demanding an eight-hour day. At intervals soldiers marched under flags printed with the one word "Land," and crying at the tops of their voices, "Peace without Annexation and Contribution."

"Da, da" (yes, yes), muttered an old moujik, tapping his neighbour on the shoulder; "that's what we want: peace without annexation and contribution."

But his friend was not so sure. He scratched his head in a puzzled way. "I don't know, comrade; I think we had better look those two places up on the map, they may be useful to Russia."

Poor, earnest old peasants, how little they understood. After the soldiers came quantities of Jews; old, bearded men, young, eager boys with dark eyes and the proverbial noses, full-bosomed women, and children, black-browed and keen-faced, singing in unison and carrying flags with Hebraic inscriptions.

And still they swept on in crowds; more women, more workmen, children, youths, and soldiers. Many of them wore national costume, making a wonderful splash of colour on a dusty road. Nurses came in ambulance carts with crippled soldiers. Mounted Cossacks rode up, and once a cart passed containing a group of children in fancy dress - a tableau representing Russia freed from the yoke of oppression. It was all very strange and touching.

Perhaps half of them did not realize the meaning of the word "Liberty," but, then, who does? One thing was obvious: that these people, so long oppressed by autocracy, trusted one another and forgave their enemies, for marching with them were a number of Austrian socialists, unguarded prisoners who rejoiced with the multitude. A few stragglers followed, principally old men, and children in red frocks who were for ever being snatched from the gutter, and then, striding along as though they had bought the earth, their rags fluttering in the wind, their old sheepskin hats planted at the backs of their heads, came some thirty or forty unshaved rascals under the scarlet legend: "The Committee of THIEVES greets the Russian Republic."

CHAPTER IV
A Criminal's Paradise

THE FIRST THING that the revolutionaries did when they were definitely sure that the old regime had been destroyed was to open the jail doors and let out all the prisoners. Not only were political offenders liberated, but habitual criminals, condemned for petty larceny, robbery, and arson. The streets were crowded with these starved, evil-looking creatures, and the number of beggars increased to such an extent that it was impossible to take a walk without being followed by at least three at a time. Many of them were obviously in great distress, and they sat on the pavements or on the steps outside the church, crossing themselves whenever anyone passed, and moaning. If they were suffering from a paralysed leg or twisted arm, the limb was uncovered so that all could see the cause of their misery. Some of them left their coats unfastened exposing open sores on their breasts, and in the intervals of praying God to bless those who gave them money, they ate sunflower seeds and spat the husks into the road till one felt that the air must be thick with germs.

There was no law to cope with the beggars, and they were not helped by the town. Many of them were quite wealthy, but were so used to the life that they could not "retire." After the downfall of the police they increased rapidly, and among them were quantities of children sent out by their parents who either could not or would not work. Certainly these babies were most attractive. They were brown as berries and bright as buttons, and they always ran up and down the paths, one hand outstretched for alms and the other clutching at garments which were so big that they were for ever falling off. Many of them were little Armenians.

"Bejentzé, barishnia bejentzé" (refugees, miss, refugees), they used to cry. "Give us a copeck-just a little one."

They had a fantastic language of their own, and paid one the most delightful compliments.

"Give me a copeck, my little golden princess."

"Chocolate-lady, chocolate-lady, give me something."

"The sweet-smelling pearl won't go away without giving something to the bejentzé."

"My marmalade child, give me a copeck"; and the longer one kept them waiting the more extravagant their phrases became.

Once I refused to have anything to do with a dirty little urchin who had run along by the carriage and stood on the step for quite ten minutes while a steady flow of compliments issued from his lips. Finally he grew tired and jumped to the ground. "Tfuh tarakan" (black beetle), he cried; "you are only a bourguika after all."

At this time the attitude to the bourgeoisie was undergoing a very marked change, and to be called a "bourguika" was considered by the populace an insult. Apparently anyone who wore a hat instead of the shawl affected by the peasants was in this category; and if one were well-dressed, a walk through a poor quarter of the town was often most embarrassing, as one had to run the gauntlet of scornful eyes, and hear prophecies of one's abject condition when the bourgeoisie would be crying for mercy. I began to wonder whether the Sabaroffs were not very unwise to dress so expensively and to appear so obviously wealthy, but they laughed, saying that the "simple people" were too stupid to attack the bourgeoisie and would be afraid to rise in a body in Rostov, which was a Cossack town. Even those people, who were beginning to foresee difficulties, put their trust in the Cossacks, and when the news from the Front continued to be bad they always maintained that the Cossacks at least would be faithful, and that they would force the soldiers to carry out Russia's obligations.

In spite of the Sabaroffs' incredulity, however, the feeling against the bourgeoisie was very obviously increasing. Secret meetings were held in the town, reports of which leaked out by degrees, and it became generally known that resolutions had been passed advocating the extermination of capitalists, and mentioning by name certain families in the town. The Sabaroffs and their relations, the Popoffs, were continually being cited, as they were by far the richest people in Rostov, and when I drove with Natasha in the town and turned my head I sometimes saw fists shaken at our retreating carriage. Once when we were playing tennis, some workmen climbed on to the wall and threw a brick at us.

"Their houses are cemented with the blood of the people," said the orators, and yet the Sabaroffs and the Popoffs had done much good in the town by providing free meals for the students and giving large donations to the hospitals and orphanages. Little by little these secret meetings ceased, and matters prejudicial to the interests of the bourgeoisie were discussed in the public gardens; families which the people hoped to attack were threatened, houses shortly to be pillaged were indicated; and it was openly boasted that the streets of Rostov should be "washed with blood." The markets were haunts of advanced revolutionaries, and the servants were perpetually returning with extravagant stories, which, though they were only half believed, gave rise to considerable anxiety.

An increase of crime added to the difficulties, and night-watchmen refused to guard houses unless they were given revolvers, because they feared to be overpowered by the bands of miscreants who went about committing highway robberies and breaking into shops. Thefts even took place in the main streets while people calmly looked on, afraid to expostulate and not knowing to whom they should apply for help. Many of the townsmen rather foolishly mistrusted the melitz, who had taken the place of the imperial gendarmerie, and cases, when intervention from this body would have been advisable, were very often left unreported. Ladies, wearing handsome furs, were sometimes quietly stopped and relieved of their coats before several other people, who looked on helplessly, while the robbers climbed into a cart driven by one of their gang and drove away. Thieves dressed as officers hid in lonely streets waiting for people to return from the theatre, so as to take any jewels they might happen to be wearing. Such men often had friends among the servants of the rich people, who used to warn them of the most auspicious moment for stealing.

On one occasion the church of Nahitchovan, the town adjoining Rostov, was despoiled. And on another, workmen, thinking they had found gold, tore away the brass from the statue of Catherine the Great. Early in May, 1917, jewellers were attacked so often that their shops were closed for several days and general panic prevailed. A number of students undertook police work and patrolled the streets during the early part of the evening, obliging motorists to light their lamps and to drive at a reasonable pace through the town. It was found necessary to do this as the thieves often went about in motor cars in order to escape more easily with their booty. It became rather unsafe to go out at night as the melitz, on watch for brigands, used to shoot at random, and it was impossible to know when and where they were aiming.

In the meantime the scarcity of food and other necessities increased by leaps and bounds. Sometimes the meat market was closed for a whole week. Game was bought by the rich people and their servants were given fish. This caused a great disturbance in our household, and one more crime was committed in the name of Liberty. Our cook did the marketing for the establishment, and was blamed by the servants for the lack of variety in the meals. She explained that she could not buy what did not exist, but no one believed her, and one day the coachman followed her into her room and beat her till she was badly bruised. Her cries brought Mme. Sabarova to the rescue.

She remonstrated with the coachman, whose face expressed the utmost amazement : "What, does the barinia mean to say I may not even beat her cook"—a pause—"now it is Liberty?"

Occasionally, after a universal holiday, and such holidays were frequent, there would be no bread in the town. Oil increased in price, and the commoner type of shoe was only sold to ticket-holders, who waited in queues outside the shops. The price of boots was prohibitive, and the largest shops rarely contained more than fifteen pairs. Three hundred roubles was charged to make a pair of high boots (lady's size) to order. At one time all the cinemas closed for a while owing to the shortage of coal, and when charcoal gave out we could not use the samovar for ten days. These deprivations excited the people, so that well dressed men and women became the subject of bitter comment, and when their backs were turned they were cursed.

The peasants were not sufficiently sure of themselves to grumble openly when they were not supported by a crowd; they only expressed frank rebellion at meetings attended by their own kind. They were just beginning to feel that a certain power was theirs, but they did not yet know how to use it. It seemed to me that they would always go with the tide, for if one talked with them, giving new ideas, they almost invariably agreed and were gently respectful and kind, unless they were five or six to one, when they would take the opinion of the stronger side, and I always felt that a capable minority, strong simply because it was organized, would win the support of the peasants by the mere fact that it was already arranged and easy for them to follow Drunken men, who had rarely been seen in the streets after the ban on vodka, now became more common. We used to see them reeling up the road and lying huddled about the paths asleep, or sick from whatever poisonous concoction they had been swallowing. Nobody bothered about them. The money in their pockets, and their boots, if they had any, were stolen, and they were left to sleep off the effects of their orgy, or kicked into something like wakefulness by their relatives who had come to seek them. No one knew where they obtained their intoxicating liquor, but it cannot have been difficult for them to find it as drunkenness obviously increased.

News from the Front became worse daily, and it was generally thought that the fall of Petrograd was imminent. People gave enormous sums for tickets in the south-going trains and were left on the platform. Soldiers continued to desert, and bands of them arrived in the town and wandered about the streets doing nothing. They filled the trains so that it became almost impossible to travel, particularly when "place-tickets," which had insured against overcrowding, were abolished. Soldiers swarmed into the carriages, occupied the lavatories, refusing access to them, crowded on to the upper and lower berths, climbed in at the windows, and even sat on the luggage-racks. First-class tickets exempted no one from undesirable society, and if a bourgeois occupied a place which a soldier wanted he was ordered to move. To refuse was dangerous, as the "tovarishchi" (comrades - a term by which the revolutionaries were universally known) did not hesitate to throw unwelcome passengers out of the window. Whether they were killed or not was a matter of no importance.

A CRIMINAL'S PARADISE

This, however, had its humorous side, and an acquaintance of mine described how, some months after the revolution, he travelled to Baku in a train plastered with the following notice: "Will the tovarishchi kindly refrain from throwing passengers on to the lines while the train is in motion, as it creates a bad impression abroad." People paid to have carriages reserved, but they were invariably disappointed, and arrived at their destination, bruised with jostling, ill with fatigue and starvation, and without their luggage, which had either been stolen or for which there had been no room.

The bad news from the Front caused the value of the rouble to drop, and prices rose to such an extent that shopping became a nightmare. With the rise in the cost of food, thieving increased, and it was difficult to sleep at night owing to the noise made by the melitz shooting in the streets. A party of hooligans broke into one of the ammunition magazines, killed the soldiers on guard, and distributed the weapons round the town. The bourgeoisie began to feel that the people were arming against them, that the Germans were hemming them in on all sides, and that there was no escape. They pinned their faith to Kerensky. The name was on every lip.

Everywhere the word "Kerensky" was heard, and Kerensky - talked.

CHAPTER V
A Journey and a Holiday

THE SUMMER, DUSTY and hot with continuous sunshine and no rain, made it impossible to remain in town, and people who were not afraid of travelling prepared to go to the Crimea or the Caucasus. The Sabaroffs had taken a "dacha" (country house) at Ceredny Fontan, just outside Odessa, where they hoped to join their elder daughter; but they dreaded the four-days' journey on a line frequented by troop-trains. Couriers were sent to precede them so that they should have as little difficulty as possible, and two maids were taken to wait upon them.

In spite of these arrangements the journey was most uncomfortable, as the Sabarofis, instead of travelling with as little luggage as possible, had brought numberless Japanese boxes filed with hats, blouses, and the delicate articles of clothing which they were afraid to put in the big trunks; beside a holdall apiece containing blankets and cushions. They explained that it was not possible to sleep without pillows, so that each carried two big ones and a little one for the small of her back, and looked pityingly at my one air cushion and light Jaeger rug. In addition to the Japanese boxes and the holdalls we had two large baskets of food, so that even though the all-powerful system of bribery had secured for us two first-class coupés, there was not room to move. It was stiflingly hot, as we were obliged to bolt the windows at night lest the soldiers, who never scrupled to disturb the "bourgzhui," should climb in while we were asleep.

At midnight hundreds of them boarded the train and banged at our door, which was locked. The provodnik in charge of the carriage, who had been promised a large tip, refused to admit them, whereupon they cursed him for pandering to the "pigs of bourgeoisie" and threatened to throw him out of the window. He managed to calm them, and we spent a peaceful night. The next morning we were unable to leave the coupé, as the corridors were filled with soldiers, so we spent our time reading and looking out of the window. We passed through long tracts of corn-land, woods and hills, stretches of uncultivated ground, curious little hamlets of low wooden huts and mud wigwams thatched with straw, and eventually reached Kiev several hours late.

Our courier met us, greatly distressed because he had only been able to find rooms in a second-rate hotel. We, however, were too tired to be particular, and were glad to rest anywhere outside the station. We spent an amusing evening, as Kiev was suffering from drought and so we could not have baths, and the servants, still revelling in their newly acquired liberty, refused to give us a meal because it was Sunday. Finally we bribed one of them to bring a samovar, and picnicked on tea and the remains of our provisions. I was sleepless, as Mme. S——had, the last thing at night, stuffed a bag of jewels under my mattress, assuring me they would be safer there than with her.

We breakfasted late and then took a carriage and drove all round the town and into the country beyond. The streets were broad and dusty, and here and there peasants stood crossing themselves before little shrines. Young girls in wide pleated skirts gathered in at the waist, with embroidered aprons and tight white bodices full in the sleeve, walked barefooted through the markets. Beyond the town we passed a tiny cemetery set in a tangle of wild roses, and far below the level of the road a broad river stretched, dark in places where the water was deep, and, where the shallows came, showing the sand under its surface.

Here and there the straight, nude figure of a man dived

from the bank. In the distance rafts were piloted by gaily dressed workmen, and as far as the eye could see there were fields, hamlets, and golden-domed towns. On one side of the road a high plateau towered, and here the green and white walls of a monastery were thrown into relief by the vivid summer sky. Below the plateau tall cypress trees and poplars stood motionless. The air was so still that not a leaf stirred, and it seemed as though life had, for the moment, been suspended. The grass, except where a hidden stream made it emerald, was yellow, and the landslips showed patches of thick red clay. It was a medley of wonderful colours, and above everything the blue sky gleamed like a great polished turquoise.

We felt very far away from wars and revolutions and came back to earth with a shock when we drove up to the station. The entrance was so crowded that horses thrust their noses into our Victoria, and when we found it impossible to push them out we dismounted and threaded our way among the carriages and market carts until we reached the ticket office. There was dirt and squalor everywhere, and a pungent smell of sheepskins. Soldiers in dust-coloured uniforms crowded the platforms, sleeping, eating, lounging, talking. It was difficult to pass this mass of humanity. We had to step over them, walk round them, stumble against them, and not a finger would they move to give us room to pass. Why help the bourguikas?

We stood for an hour and a half in the sun, waiting for the train. The weather was windless, and as most of the soldiers were smoking, the fumes of bad tobacco hung about in the air. Several people were sick, and it was with the utmost difficulty that I controlled an inclination to faint. When the heat became almost unbearable the train arrived, and a vast crowd surged towards it, fighting, laughing, shouting, elbowing smaller people into the background, pushing one another out of the way. Bruised with jostling, and out of breath, we struggled into our coupé and locked the door while the soldiers, linking their arms together like alpine climbers, scrambled on to the roofs of the carriages, hung on to the steps, and smashed the windows so as to be able to sit astride the casements. Second- and third-class coupés contained as many as thirty people. We slept two to a berth and never opened our door. There was no restaurant car, and refreshments were not sold at the stations, so that after feeding on tea and bread for two days we arrived at Odessa thoroughly tired and very cross.

Our dacha was situated two or three miles outside the town in a large uncultivated garden, surrounded by trees and fields, and about ten minutes' walk from the sea. It was a low, wooden bungalow, furnished with the barest necessities, as the chairs, tables, and cupboards were all newly bought for the occasion, and such things were inordinately expensive. There was an asphalt tennis court and a gravel croquet ground, and we had all our meals on the veranda. The servants' quarters were in a different building, the other side of the garden path and over the kitchen and laundry, and they had to carry the meals across to our house.

All the time we were there we found it very difficult to procure meat, and so lived on chicken, duck, and fish, all of which were very dear. We spent from forty to fifty roubles* a day on dinner only, and this was considered a great deal, though later in the year we thought nothing of it. Butter was eight roubles a pound; water melons, which before the war could have been bought for five copecks apiece, were now two

---

* Pre-war value of a rouble about 2s. 1d. † One hundred copecks = one rouble. *These figures reveal the dramatic impact of inflation. One rouble, equivalent to just over 10p (2s. 1d) in 1917, would have the purchasing power of around £6 in 2025 values. So the family are spending today's equivalent of £250-300 on food for dinner, £50 for a pound of butter, £40 for a pound of tea and £12 for a water melon that would have cost 30p before the War. Figures based on the Bank of England Inflation Calculator. See also Chapter VI.* BP

roubles each; the best tea was seven roubles a pound, and wood, which had been twenty-five roubles per cartload the preceding year, had risen to a hundred and fifty roubles.

We lived entirely on the estate, rarely going into the town, but occasionally making expeditions to distant villages. Once we walked across the fields to a disused garden where we gathered blue speedwell and little pink "everlastings." A peasant woman who prepared hot water for us, stood at her cottage door, with children clinging to her skirts, and watched us eating. She kissed our hands when we gave her what was left of the provisions, and followed us down the road, crying and asking God to send us happiness. On our way back we passed a gipsy encampment, where nut-brown children, so ragged that they were scarcely covered, sprawled in the dust. The grey carts and caravans were massed together to form a rough shelter, and the women were cooking over fires and eating out of the same pot with long wooden spoons. As we passed, the dogs, tied under the carts, strained at the ropes, and barked. Simultaneously the men burst into a fantastic song, accompanied by a little three-cornered stringed instrument.

Dusk was falling, and the flickering firelight cast long shadows on the ground, and showed the wild gipsy faces, weird and almost inhuman. I wanted to stay and listen, but the men of the party hurried us on. They were all armed, but it was getting dark and they thought it safer for us to be indoors.

We used to bathe every morning in the sea, swimming a little way out to avoid mingling with the naked women who had discarded their bathing dresses when once in the water. Those of them who preferred not to be completely unclothed wore short coloured shirts, believing them to be more hygienic than the stockinette "tricot." The greater number, however, lay about on the sand or in the water quite naked, their idea being that if they covered themselves people would think they were suffering from some physical defect. Of course the bathing-place was a little apart, but it was easily visible from the hotel windows and from "Arcadia," the haunt of holiday makers, who sat watching the swimmers and sipping iced lemonade.

The summer holiday was looked upon by the Sabaroffs as a sort of rest-cure, and they spent most of the day lying in long chairs under the trees and sleeping from four to six. The days were very hot, so that most people got up late and did not go to bed until after midnight. We had numberless tea-parties to celebrate birth- and name-days, and when the guests had arrived in the garden Natasha used to take me to the window and point out the different families, giving a brief but comprehensive sketch of their personal history and adding original notes on their love affairs.

"Little Spider, you see the man with the big moustache - he who is so ugly? His lovair is his chambermaid, and he teaches her the manicure so that when he no longer needs her she will not starve. It is an idea, hein? We have her for our hands when we are here. It pleases him. And that pretty lady with the so-rouged lips; it is Baroness X — Of the three men with her - the tall he is her husband (she divorced an old man for him), and the two others are her lovairs."

"You talk a surprising amount of nonsense, Natasha — nobody in her five senses would take both her lovers and her husband to a party. It—well, anyhow, it's not done."

"English one, you are now in Russia. But even so, I, too, think she makes an error. The husband, he is a convenience, the lovair a necessity - but two lovairs, surely that is a luxury."

All this time great anxiety was felt as to the result of the revolution upon the war. Brussilov's splendid offensive had temporarily raised people's hopes, but when it became known that the soldiers had all straggled back to the old trenches and were holding meetings to decide whether they should carry out their officers' orders or not, they realized that for a while Russia could no longer be said to be making war. The fall of Riga came as a shock to many people who still hoped that the soldiers would rally round the officers.

Later in the year we had a Polish cook who had escaped in a miraculous manner from this town, and she gave us a long account of what had happened. How true it was I do not know, but it was extraordinarily vivid. She told how, when most of the soldiers had left the town, aeroplanes were sent up to destroy the bridges. Enemy aeroplanes were also active, so that many houses caught fire and the inhabitants rushed about the streets. The bombs made great craters in the roads and many people were killed. At nightfall all was dark except in places where the houses were burning. The noise was so great that when the church tower fell the crash was indistinguishable.

In the midst of this the enemy launched a gas attack, and men, women, and children fell about the roads, choking and suffocated. Many were buried in the shell holes. The gates and walls of the Zoological Gardens were destroyed, and the wild beasts, terrified, broke loose and rushed into the town. Children were violated by the soldiers, who were, in many cases, drunk. Gold and silver were stolen, furniture burnt. "It was hell, barishnia," said Paulina, crying.

The attitude towards the Kerensky-Korniloff affair was not unanimous.

Many people thought that the combined efforts of these leaders would relieve the situation, and were utterly appalled when they suddenly discovered that the two were in opposite camps. Others knew Korniloff to be a strong and popular man, but were convinced that a military dictatorship would lead to further dissension in the country, and that the people who had just burst their bonds would stand nothing that savoured so strongly of militarism. At the time the situation was extremely

A JOURNEY AND A HOLIDAY

difficult to grasp. News, even from within the country, was very long in coming through, and when it did arrive the accounts were so garbled and the versions of what was happening so contradictory that no one could get a clear idea of the position.

In the meantime the minor disorders, due to lack of organization and a definite controlling body, were increasing rapidly. The environs of Odessa appeared to be entirely unprotected. Thieving, and even murder, were common, and we were perpetually being awakened at night by cries and shots. The fruit in our orchard was stolen nightly, the flowers uprooted, and any chairs or articles such as the tennis net, left in the garden overnight, had always disappeared by the next morning. Our guardian, a short, thick-set man of about forty, with a low type of head and brutal expression, was continually frightening us with tales of what went on in the neighbourhood. We did not trust him, but as he lived at the lodge and we could get no one in his place we were obliged to keep him. The following notes from my diary will show the state of lawless-ness in the town during July and August:

July 26th. Awakened by screams and shots. Two thieves entered the bungalow next door and stole clothes and plate. Grigori, the watchman, saw them come into our garden.

July 27th. Awakened by shooting near the house and the barking of our watchdog.

July 28th. We sat up late, as the moon was bright, and did not attempt to go to bed until after midnight. At about two o'clock in the morning I was awakened by cries of "Thief" and "Murder" under my window. I waited for a moment, listening intently. The cries redoubled, and came from the other side of the house. The dogs barked furiously and shots were fired. I ran into the passage, where the rest of the family had congregated. It appears that Grigori had slept while on guard and had awakened to find two men on the veranda. Stealthily creeping round till he came to the other side of the house he had hoped to get help, but, to his alarm, ran into two more, one in the act of effecting an entrance through my bedroom window. A scuffle ensued, and shots were fired, the cries from the next-door garden and the howls of neighbouring dogs adding to the confusion. The thieves escaped, but there was no more sleep for us.

July 29th. Grigori arrived, complaining bitterly that his revolver would not work. He was given our one and only weapon, which he tested and pocketed. After measuring us with his eye for a moment he quietly informed us that he had no intention of guarding the house again and calmly walked away with our only fire-arm lying snugly in his pocket. At night I woke hearing stealthy footsteps on the gravel under my window-in the morning we found all the pears had been stolen.

July 30th. This morning we were told that men broke into our neighbour's house and cut the throats of three people before making off with money and clothes.

July 31st. Artillery practice appeared to take place in the garden last night.

August 2nd. More shooting at night.

August 5th. Mme. M—'s daughter-in-law has had everything of value in her house stolen.

August 6th. A lady living in the neighbourhood left the bathing-place unaccompanied. When half-way up the hill she was overtaken by two soldiers, one of whom pinioned her while the other divested her of her brooch and necklace, after which they thanked her and walked away as if nothing had happened.

And so it went on week after week until it even became unsafe to wander about by day, and whenever we wanted to go for walks we either went in a large party or in couples, followed by an armed man. In Odessa itself disorders of this kind were not so prevalent, as there were too many people. Speeches were made in the streets, and once we saw a party of Austrian prisoners holding a well-attended peace meeting. There was a good deal of illness, due chiefly to the difficulty of obtaining wholesome food, and when cholera broke out we made preparations to go home, only remaining for the baptism of Mme. Sabarova's grandson, a quaint ceremony to which the priest forgot to come and was sought by an agitated godfather all round the town. He was eventually found, and, after prayers and prostrations, immersed the child in a bowl of water and finally cut off a lock of its hair. Those present then processed round the font with lighted candles, and afterwards adjourned to the dining-room for a champagne supper.

Our return journey to Rostov was uneventful and tiring. The train was of course crowded with soldiers, but heavy bribes secured us a coupé to ourselves. We could not sleep owing to the noisy soldiers, the lack of space, and the raids made upon us by bugs, which infested the carriage. Food could not be bought on the way, and the soldiers played havoc with the property of the railway, breaking of the metal fittings, stealing the brass taps, and converting the plush cushions into strips for puttees. We were lucky to have been travelling in so big a party, otherwise we should have shared the discomfort of other passengers and been obliged to submit to discourtesy and even robbery.

CHAPTER VI
An Autumn of Anxiety

AUTUMN FOUND US once more in Rostov full of late roses and chrysanthemums, and the yard noisy with poultry. Warnings of an approaching famine had caused prudent people to lay in a good supply of chickens, ducks, and geese, which were daily rising in value. Most necessary articles were seven times as expensive as they had been in the spring, and the sugar and meat allowances per head had been reduced to one pound a month and three-quarters of a pound a week respectively. It was not, however, always possible to buy as much as this, and shortly afterwards the allowance was still further decreased. Mediocre soap was seven roubles a cake, perfumes from a hundred roubles a bottle. Material was so scarce that we had tickets for clothes, and were allowed to buy only one new blouse for the winter.

Woollen stuff, poor in quality, cost from fifty to a hundred roubles an arsheen (about three-quarters of a yard), and ready-made costumes did not exist. High boots, made to order, could not be purchased under five hundred roubles a pair, and for sixty roubles repairs were badly executed. Leather was scarce and rubber was used in its place. Simple hats made with inferior materials cost at least a hundred roubles, and it was so difficult to get food for the horses that isvoschiks (cab drivers) trebled their fares. The depreciation of the rouble forced up the prices of everything, and for ten gold roubles a hundred paper ones were given. Shopkeepers sometimes refused the new paper money, and in many of the villages round Rostov the peasants resorted to the old custom of exchange and barter, giving apples and grain for clothing, or worn implements for boots.

The shortage of food was not remedied by the ticket system, because the shopkeepers, provided they had a supply in hand, charged the rich people what they pleased. This angered the peasants, who, although they were earning good wages, could not get meat, simply because the butchers saved all the best morsels for their wealthy customers, reserving for the poor people the bony portion of cows' heads, which was often so rotten that it smelt bad, and for which they asked sixty copecks a pound. Pogroms were threatened, and one wet day, when the rain fell in a depressing drizzle, some fifty or sixty women marched through the town, one of them carrying a cow's head on a pole. They shook their fists at it, crying, "This is the poor man's meat," "Give us cheap food." The wind blew their wet skirts against their legs, outlining their forms, and long strands of hair escaped from under their shawls. They were grimly determined, and one felt that the patient resignation with which they had been used to bear their troubles had at last disappeared.

Meetings continued to be held at all points, and the rich bourgeoisie were distinctly nervous. Servants began to leave, and when pressed for a reason always gave the same reply, "The tovarishchi say it is dangerous, and that very soon the house will be blown up." Hardly a week passed without our hearing something of this kind, and our watchman took to sitting behind a locked gate instead of outside, as he was continually being threatened by masked men. Once or twice some of the big shops were guarded by the melitz, and threats of pogroms became so frequent that the Sabaroffs hired a flat in Novocherkask, whither they hoped to escape when it was dangerous. Novocherkask, being the capital of the Don Cossacks, was supposed to be safer than Rostov, which was beginning to show a tendency towards Bolshevism.

The atmosphere of the town had changed since the spring, and "Liberty" was running riot. During the month of October we did not know whether we were standing upon our heads or our heels, and I felt as though I were living in the middle of a "shilling shocker." Not a character in the plot was omitted, from the masked villain to the blackmailed father and kidnapped child, and the difficulties were due chiefly to the release of prisoners from the jails. Realizing that the melitz had very little power, and that they were not likely to be arrested, these people united, forming various societies which undertook to terrorize the rich townsmen by writing anonymous letters demanding immense sums and threatening vengeance if their wishes were left unfulfilled. It was all very childish, but very unpleasant.

There was the Union of ex-Criminals, the Society of the Red Hand, and the Committee of Adventurers and Apaches. Several people received letters which contained threats to murder them or bomb their houses, and, terrified beyond measure, paid the money demanded, saying nothing to their friends. This encouraged the criminals, and so many families received anonymous letters that the matter became really serious. One of the townsmen who had had several such epistles was called up by telephone and asked by the Apaches what he intended to do. His reply was brief: "Send you to the devil," he said, ringing off. But he left the town for a couple of days, and one night his house was bombed.

Shortly afterwards, Monsieur Krasnov, a well-known merchant, who was unpopular among his own employees, received a similar note. He refused to reply, and was threatened both by letter and by telephone. In the meantime Monsieur Sabaroff also had a note which had been handed to his servant by a sailor. It was ill-spelt and couched in grandiloquent terms, written on paper headed "The Committee of Adventurers and

Apaches," decorated with the figure of a masked man, and folded in a blood-coloured envelope, on which the address and a grinning death's head were printed. Fifteen thousand roubles was demanded, and a red embroidered ribbon enclosed. The sum was to be taken one night to a certain street by a maid, who was to wear the ribbon and give the money to a man who would hand her the facsimile of an enclosed card. Refusal to comply with this request was to be followed by dire calamity. Monsieur Sabaroff sent the maid *plus* the melitz, the result of which was a telephone message, saying we would shortly see a horrible example of vengeance.

The next day another house was bombed, and we received a second letter enumerating eleven different methods by which the Apaches would take their vengeance.

"We shall not hesitate to wall up our victims," they wrote, adding, "We know you have a flat at Novocherkask, but if you flee there our members will pursue you. We have even representatives among the police."

To put our nerves still further on the rack, our watchman naïvely informed us that during the night he had been "awakened" by the dog. Peeping through a crack, he saw five masked men attempting to break into the house. He fired in the air, and they made off, shouting, "Wait till next time."

We began to get very nervous, and matters reached a climax when Monsieur Krasnov's little son was kidnapped, and the melitz came up to tell us that pogroms were expected the next day, as a meeting had been held during which the Sabaroffs had been cited as possible victims. We fled to Novocherkask in a car. I shall never forget that flight. We seemed to be carried through the air, and nothing but another car could have caught us. We could not be recognized, partly because we were going too fast and partly because we had thick veils over our faces. Our luggage was covered by a rug in case the tovarishchi should guess we were trying to escape, and we sped across the steppes, clouds of dust whirling round us, past droves of frightened sheep and processions of bearded peasants with carts.

There was something extraordinarily desolate about this region; no houses, no fields, uncultivated land for miles and miles, corpses of horses and dogs lying at intervals, sometimes in the middle, sometimes at the side of the road. Occasionally a wild-faced man leapt from behind a tufted knoll of grass and stared at us with eager eyes. Once we had a breakdown, and Mme. Sabarova trembled as the chauffeur pulled up and went under the car. In ten minutes we were off again. A motor passed us at breakneck speed, and we held our breath as three tense white faces flashed by in a cloud of grey dust. We thought we were being pursued and might be stopped before reaching Novocherkask. As we neared the town the scenery changed, and the desolation was relieved by a few isolated huts, some mills, and, in the far distance, a church with gilded domes.

We spent five days in hiding, while the situation in Rostov became more serious. Monsieur Sabaroff, who had returned after the third day, was unable to leave home unarmed and without a detective. The house was like a fortress. Armed and mounted members of the melitz rode up and down the garden all night. Detectives slept in the unused rooms, and a guard was placed in the kitchen, which looked out on to the high road. Twice the house was attacked by masked men who arrived in a motor, but who were unable to do much material damage owing to the strength of the guard.

Every day a note appeared mysteriously on the veranda or was thrown on to the garden path, or a telephone message was received. Monsieur Sabaroff tried to temporize by offering a smaller sum, but the Apaches loftily replied that their president did not see his way to considering the proposal. In

AN AUTUMN OF ANXIETY

the meantime our hiding place became known, so we returned home escorted by two Cossacks and a detective. That afternoon the town was horrified to hear that Monsieur Krasnov's little son had been found buried in a sitting position in a field. A postmortem examination showed that the child had been starved, and that death was due to strangulation. After the little boy had been kidnapped, the father had advertised, saying he would pay any sum provided the child were brought back. Six different criminal associations answered, each saying they had the child and suggesting, in every case, a different meeting-place.

The poor father did not know what to do, and the delay cost the boy his life. Reports of this appeared in the local papers, and were followed by an epidemic of anonymous letter-writing. Some children of quite poor people were kidnapped and held up for ransom, two young girls disappeared from a school, and the wife of a rich merchant who lived in Novocherkask was chloroformed in the cinema at Rostov and kept a prisoner until her husband had paid a large sum of money. A friend of Mme. Sabarova overheard in the market a plot to kidnap Natasha and her cousin, and for days we could not leave the house, and when at last we ventured to go for a short walk we were accompanied by a detective.

After some weeks' anxiety the melitz succeeded in running our tormentors to earth, and they were imprisoned. Every one knew, however, that events were moving with such rapidity that all criminals would again be liberated and that this precautionary measure would not even afford a temporary respite, because other societies were still active. Indeed, anonymous letters continued to arrive, and even poor workmen were robbed and threatened. Though these weeks were nerve-wearing, they were, at times, very amusing, and we were so unstrung that anything, however remotely funny, gave us food for laughter.

IN THE STORM

Our gardener's son disappeared, shortly after the death of the little Krasnov. The parents were frantic and sought him everywhere. The mother went to the melitz headquarters daily, weeping for her "little pigeon." For a week there was no sign of the child, and when we had given up all hope, and the father had burnt a candle for him in the parish church, a disappointed little figure, dusty and forlorn, slunk in by the back door, saying it was no good playing Robinson Crusoe in Rostov because there were no goats to kill.

Hardly a day passed without either a murder or a robbery, and such crimes were almost invariably committed in well-frequented streets, and often in the big hotels, where it was probable that porters were bribed by the brigands to leave the doors unguarded. The people in the hotels were accosted by these armed and masked villains and forced to lie on their faces on the floor while wholesale robbery took place. They were obliged to give up money and jewels, and on one occasion three English officers happened to be dining at an hotel which was attacked in this way. The robbers were very polite. They had no quarrel with foreigners, but they must request the Englishmen to be so kind as to get under the table. The Englishmen lit their pipes and obeyed. They could do nothing else.

Workmen and soldiers warned the servants in our house that bombs were going to be thrown, and that the Sabaroffs ("pigs of bourgzhui") would soon cease to exist. The watchman left, as every night the shooting in our street increased and it was not safe to walk up and down in front of the house. We engaged people from the melitz to stand on guard night and day, but they were perpetually being threatened with death and so arranged to be on duty in pairs. After a while crimes perpetrated by masked men became so monotonous that we shrugged our shoulders when we heard of them, and continued to lead as normal a life as possible, taking care, however, never to go out at night unaccompanied by an armed man.

While this lawlessness increased, events of political importance were taking place, and one night in November, after the Kerensky government had been overthrown and the Bolshevik riots had spread from Petrograd to Moscow, a large meeting of workmen was held in one of the Rostov committee rooms. A friend of Mme. Sabarova attended it, disguised as a peasant, and afterwards described the disorder and the temper of the crowd. One man was hooted down to the cries of "Traitor" for saying, "Comrades, let us keep our hands free from blood." Fists were shaken in his face and he was spat upon, and sailors, said to have arrived from Sebastopol with a view to stirring up strife between the Bolsheviks and the Cossacks, drove him from the hall. A delegate from the north declared that very little fighting had taken place in Petrograd, but that events had been exaggerated by the bourgeoisie with a view to disgusting the people and making the Bolsheviks unpopular. This was greeted by shouts of "Never," booing and hissing, and the meeting broke up with cries of "Down with the bourgeoisie."

Rumours from Moscow became more disquieting, and unrest in Rostov culminated in a detachment of the local Red Guard attempting to seize the Post Office. Cossacks armed with guns and whips drove them off. Both sides were good-humoured and looked upon the whole thing as a joke, but the incident was too significant to be treated lightly, and Kaledin, who was then Ataman of the Don district, put the town under martial law.

The elections, for which there was no canvassing, resulted in a gain for the Bolsheviks at Rostov and for the Cossacks at Novocherkask. It was rumoured at the time that Cossack regiments had returned from the Front, and that in the event of a separate peace, to which the Bolsheviks might, through force of circumstances, be obliged to agree, they would declare the Don district a separate republic. Every one was waiting for something to happen, but what the something was nobody seemed to know. At the moment Rostov was neither fish, fowl, nor good red herring. The Ataman had placed the town under martial law, but the Bolsheviks had won the election. It was something like the riddle of the irresistible force which met the immovable mass. Nobody could guess the result.

CHAPTER VII
Civil War

BOOM! A SHELL BURST on the steppes sending a shower of dust and stones into the air. Down the road armed men were marching, some of them mere boys, the "rag-tag and bob-tail" of the gutter, who formed the local section of the Red Guard. Marching? Well, perhaps that conveys an impression of double files and formed fours. Straggling would be a better word. Some were hurrying, some loitering, others shuffling through the gutter. They were all laughing, and every now and then one raised his gun and shot into the air. Peasant women with startled eyes peered from their cottage windows. Here and there a young girl ran through the door and mingled with the crowd, chaffing first one and then another, and dexterously avoiding the proffered kisses. If these men had not been carrying guns they might have been going to a picnic. They seemed so irresponsible and jolly. At each new crash they shouted "Hurrah!" and some of them began to run.

We did not know what had happened, nor how this long-smouldering fire had burst into flame; we only heard the heavy booming of the cannon and the sharp, irritating rattle of the machine guns. I put on an old coat, and, twisting a shawl round my head to avoid looking like a "bourguika," stole into the garden and listened. Snow was falling, and a thin film had settled on the path. The air was bitterly cold. I pulled back the bolt which secured the big iron gate against the intrusion of unwelcome visitors, and slipped into the road. The detonation of the guns shook the windows in the houses, and the battle seemed to be quite near if not actually in Rostov. The tovarishchi had passed and I kept a little way behind them, covering the lower part of my face with the shawl so as not to be recognized by the moujiks who knew me. Old men were talking in groups, and I gathered that Nahitchovan was being shelled and that perhaps Rostov would be destroyed. I did not know why, and as no one seemed any wiser than myself I hurried on. At the corner of the main street there was a cannon, and beyond that another. An armoured car shunted along, and carts filled with furniture and sand-bags were passing in the direction of the station.

"What has happened, tovarish?" I asked a soldier who was guarding the street corner.

"Patotski is fighting."

"But why? It was quiet yesterday."

"He arrested the Bolshevik leader and now there is Civil War."

"Well, but which soldiers are fighting ?"

"The Red Guard. We must kill the Junkers and Cadets."

"And the Cossacks?"

He threw me a quick glance and looked away. "How should I know? Go home, barishnia, you'll be hurt" - and I could get nothing more out of him.

The word "Cossacks" seemed to have sealed his lips, and apparently he had no idea whether they were with Patotski or against him. This seemed a little strange. It was a well-known fact that the bourgeoisie was relying upon Cossack help, and here was a man, obviously about to take part in a battle, who did not know, or preferred not to say, on whose side the Cossacks were fighting. It certainly gave one food for thought, and I went home wondering whether we were as safe in the Don district as we had imagined.

I found the Sabaroffs packing, and in a highly nervous state. Mme. Sabaroff was crying, and Monsieur rushing up and down, telephoning orders and counter-orders. The whole household was in a ferment. Natasha, lying on her sofa, sulked.

"Litle Spider, dear. If you only knew how borded (bored) I am. Father is angry as if I was a Bolshevik, and mother she cries. I wished to play halma with Fräulein, and she said 'Gott behüte.' But it is impossible."

It was useless to discuss the affair with any one of them. They were all too upset to answer questions, and their one idea, regardless of the fact that the rails might be destroyed, was to leave the town by train and take refuge in Novocherkask.

The whole day the battle raged round Nahitchovan, and at night the machine guns kept us awake. The next morning there was a short respite, and we drove through back streets and alleys towards the station. This was a thoroughly unpleasant experience. Soldiers, roaring with laughter, wished us a prosperous journey. Peasant women and girls shouted at us, calling their neighbours to come and see the rich people running away. To make matters worse, when we reached the station we were told that the trains were not leaving Rostov, and so we had to return and listen to their jeering remarks about our "short holiday." When we arrived at our gates we found the watchman had left everything unlocked, and a crowd of moujiks surrounded our carriage, asking us whether we knew that perhaps one day we should have no house, and had therefore better take advantage of it while we could, and not attempt to go away.

Thus the day began badly, and everything combined to make it as unpleasant as possible. We were warned that the Bolsheviks might try to cut off the water supply and so filled every available vessel, including the bath. We had no meat in the house and prepared to lunch on kasha (a sort of porridge), but our meal was disturbed by a terrific hammering on the garden gate. Natasha and I ran to the window and saw that the house was surrounded by about two hundred men, some in uniform, some in ordinary clothes, and all armed. As we looked, a number of them climbed on to the roof, dropped into the garden, and swarmed up the veranda steps.

To prevent them from breaking the glass panes, Monsieur Sabaroff went out to meet them. His wife was trembling. "They will kill us," she said, and burst into tears. We tried to calm her, but we were all very much frightened, and the fact that our own servants had wandered into the yard and were in earnest conversation with the intruders did not mend matters. They seemed to have a leader, a tall, bearded creature in a fur coat and a slouch hat, who reminded me irresistibly of the villain in an East End melodrama. He stood with his head thrown back and his legs apart, denouncing us in the orthodox villain's way, and the crowd advanced with fixed bayonets.

"You are hiding Cossacks here," he said.

Fräulein murmured something about this being an "Unsinn," and he turned upon her furiously. "That woman," he shouted, "has been seen by me and others driving in a motor with Cossack officers. She and this household are against the people."

We expostulated, and the servants watched us out of the corners of their eyes. The bayonets advanced perceptibly, and the leader called upon us to show our motor. Now, the car was tyreless and had not been out since the spring, but he promptly identified it as the machine which had been used by Cossack officers. The crowd shouted angrily and demanded the car, which we said they could take away at once. We would have given anything to have seen them safely off the premises, and hoped that they would take the car and go. They remained, however, for twenty minutes arguing among themselves, and finally marched away announcing that they would return at midnight to search the house for the Cossacks, whom they still maintained were in the cellar.

CIVIL WAR

Our one idea was to get rid of them definitely at all costs, so we offered to take them over the house immediately, but this seemed to amuse them, and laughing among themselves they passed through the gate and away towards the steppes. We were worried and a little unnerved, for we knew that if this had been a search party by an authentic body it would have looked for the hypothetic Cossacks immediately instead of postponing the matter till midnight, when they would have had time to escape.

The men were obviously brigands who wished to profit by the abnormal conditions and had thought of this ruse to ransack a wealthy merchant's house. We had not the slightest idea how to act, and the Sabaroffs, who were naturally in great distress, retired to the drawing-room with Natasha to consider what they had better do. They were absent for a long while, and I, thinking we ought to decide quickly, went to find them. I met them at the veranda door, dressed in their shoobas (overcoats) and with shawls round their heads. They smiled. "Goodbye, Miss Power; we shall come back when all is quiet. For you and Fräulein it is safe. You are foreign subjects" - and they went down the steps into the street, guarded by the melitz.

We were foreign subjects, Fräulein and I, and if these men who had arrived in the morning had been official representatives of the Government we might have been safe. But they were brigands, and we could not imagine how we should cope with them if they arrived in force. We had three male servants and two members of the melitz in the house. The servants might be discounted. They would probably open the gates for a share of the booty. We, with two men, could do nothing before a mob. We bolted the doors and waited, brewing strong tea to keep us awake. Night fell, and the noise of the guns never ceased. Shells seemed to be passing over the house. They gave a sort of shriek. The battle sounded nearer than it had done the day before.

At ten o'clock four soldiers tapped at the gate. They asked for our car, which we said they could have, but they only looked at it and went away. Five different societies arrived, one after another; each demanded the car and was given permission to take it away. It remained in the garage, for none of them could drive. At one time three men ordered us to let them into the house, and when we refused they shook their fists and stormed at us, threatening to break down the door. In the midst of this tempest the cook and coachman came up from the kitchen, shouting, "Come to the yard, tovarishchi, we'll let you in. Here there is white flour and sugar. The bourgzhui have cakes every day."

"Curse you!" cried the men, battering at the door, "there's a queue of two hundred women in this road, and they've waited six hours for bread."

The melitz strolled out. They were dressed as soldiers and they calmed the men, pretending to be with them, so that they finally went away grumbling. We returned to our strong tea and waited for the brigands.

At midnight a noise took us again to the door. We looked through the crack and recognized a crowd of uniformed melitz who had apparently rushed up on bicycles, on horses, and on foot.

"Open the door, barishnia," they cried, and we let them in. "Where is the master?"

"He is away"

"But you ought not to be here alone. It is dangerous."

"We have two guards."

"It is not enough. We have just had a warning that a band of robbers are on their way to destroy this house."

"What shall we do?"

"I don't know. We can give you very little help. Last night sixty armed men in uniform, with official passes, made us give up nearly all our guns and ammunition, ostensibly for headquarters. Later headquarters denied having sent such a convoy. It was a hoax and we can now do very little."

We begged some of them to stay, and they arranged to patrol the street, which was narrow. We were up all night listening to the revolver shots, which warned us that our sentinels were busy. In the morning we found holes in the plaster of the walls, and splashes of blood on the snow.

For two days the fighting continued. We were cut off from all communication. The telephones had ceased working, the trains were not running, and newspapers were neither published nor delivered. Once a party of Cossacks came down the main street in trams, flying the white flag. It was rumoured that all the fighting was being done by the Junkers, and that Patotski had been taken prisoner by the Bolsheviks because his soldiers had been too drunk to carry out his orders. That evening two hooligans, reeling up the hill, stopped in front of our house and, putting their heads through the kitchen window, which looked out on to the road, shouted, "What, are these pigs still alive? We thought we'd finished them off; we must speak to the Soviet about that."

On the third day there was an armistice, and the Cossacks held a conference at Novocherkask. I strolled through the town. Everything was quiet and very few people were about. Ambulance carts, full of wounded, passed in and out of the hospital gates. Women and children in cabs or walking with large bundles, struggled against the wind. Nahitchovan was being evacuated by those who had lost their homes, and these melancholy little parties came through Rostov hourly.

People were very quietly dressed, many of them having substituted shawls for hats and old coats for the fashionable shoobas, so as not to appear quite so conspicuous. Most of the shops were still shut, but the markets had opened and they were visited by a continuous procession of cooks, who were prudently laying in a stock of provisions, as it was thought that the fighting might go on for weeks if the Bolsheviks were reinforced from Petrograd.

I wandered through the town until I reached the street where the melitz headquarters were situated, and as I turned the corner a number of soldiers, shouting "Out of the way, out of the way," charged up the road shooting.

They dashed into the melitz building and remained there for some time.

"What has happened, golubchik (little dove)?" I asked a cab-driver who sat unmoved on his box.

"Oh! it is the Red Guard. They have arrested the melitz, who are most of them thieves."

I thought nervously of the two guards who had been left in charge of our house, and, going into a friend's flat, watched the proceedings from a window. Ten minutes later another detachment of soldiers rushed round the corner, acting in precisely the same way as the first. I ran downstairs into the road.

"What is it this time, golubchik?"

"Ah! it is the Red Guard, and they arrested the arresters, who are thieves." He looked affectionately at the wreckage he called a horse, and added, chucking his reins as the animal turned back one ear, "I have been speaking with my horse about it, and he says, 'Wonderful things are happening nowadays, little master, wonderful things.'"

Apparently the first arrest was a hoax on the part of a number of brigands who wished to put an end to all surveillance in the town and so have a clear field for robbery. It reminded me of Clown and Pantaloon in the pantomimes of my childhood, when the policemen always appeared at the least convenient moment, saying, "Slap-bang, here we are again!"

The armistice lasted for two days, after which the fighting began again with renewed vigour, and Zeler, the mayor of the town, was arrested by the Red Guard and conveyed to the man-of-war on the river, where Patotski was supposed to have been imprisoned. The bombardment was heavy, but seemed to be down by the station, so that it was possible to walk in the back streets provided one kept away from the road leading to the railway.

The town presented a curious aspect. Not a Red Guard or peasant was to be seen, but everywhere Cossacks, mounted and on foot, patrolled the streets. They were massed, in the fields beyond the Don. They paraded the highways. Officers walked quickly towards the station in earnest conference one with another. The Sadovaya (the main street in Rostov) was guarded on either side, and the trams were filled with Cossack soldiers. After about three-quarters of an hour the bombardment ceased altogether and more Cossacks arrived. They seemed to be in possession of the town, yet this was hardly credible as there had been so little fighting since the armistice. It was true, however, for the Red Guard, when confronted by the well-disciplined Cossack troops, had surrendered to a man, throwing down their guns and giving up their ammunition.

In a short while the news was all over the town, and the bourgeoisie, furred and jewelled, rushed into the Sadovaya to greet the victorious army.

"Hurrah! hurrah!" echoed from every corner. The pavements were crowded with enthusiasts, but here and there discontent showed plainly upon a workman's face, and some of the peasant women were crying. One old crone, standing behind us, muttered fiercely, "You can wear your new hats again now. You needn't be afraid"; and when I was going home in the dusk some moujiks spat at me and shouted "Bourguika!"

Song after song the Cossacks sang, cheer after cheer greeted Kaledin, who was at the station reading a proclamation from his car. But among the lusty singers there was a number of youths sulking, standing at attention, refusing to join in the chorus. The older men shrugged their shoulders, and a whisper was passed from lip to lip that many of the young Cossacks had refused to fight against the Bolsheviks and had been beaten through the streets by their parents. Then we wondered how long this so-called Cossack triumph would last.

CHAPTER VIII
Under Cossack Protection

THE GROUND WAS covered with a thin coating of snow, but there had been a thaw during the night, so that the gutters were filled with muddy water, rushing down from the steppes with a speed which prevented its being frozen in spite of the intense cold of the morning. A biting wind swept across the town towards the Don, and the grey sky predicted rain. Everything looked dirty and cold. Peasant women, their heads bent to meet the wind and their coloured shawls clasped tightly under their chins, walked quickly down the hill towards the church. The tolling of the bell was scarcely audible. Its sound was carried across the river by the winds, and the sombre booming could only be heard during a momentary lull. It was the burial day of the Bolsheviks, of the men, young and old, who had fallen in the struggle wherein both sides had sought to fulfil the ideal of Liberty and had died, each for freedom, yet each bitterly hating the other.

The procession started from the church, wound its way slowly through the town, and then passed up the hill to the cemetery across the steppes. At its head came a regiment of soldiers. Most of their faces were impassive. It seemed as though they were mentally shrugging their shoulders at the scene which, for them at least, was monotonous. After them, carrying wooden and iron crosses, decorated with embroidered cloths, walked the churchmen in white tunics, followed by the long-haired priests in vestments, crimson and peacock-blue. The friends and relatives of the dead, an almost unending throng, marched slowly behind the priests. They were not in mourning, and they carried laurel wreaths and flowers and little baskets of food to be given to the beggars at the cemetery gates, who would pray for the souls of the dead. Some of the old people were crying quite freely, but the young ones, with shoulders thrown back, set faces, and eyes which seemed to see some thing beyond the dim horizon, marched steadily, purpose in every movement.

One young girl with a pale, haggard face threw a look behind her, then turned and shook her fist at a green-gabled house with windows discreetly veiled, shouting fiercely: "Ha! peep through your curtains, bourgzhui. Watch the dead on their last journey; jog, jog, jog over the stones. Each coffin an enemy less, but our turn will come. We too shall be nourished by blood."

She began to laugh and scream. A boy put his arm round her and led her gently away. The crowd, still watching the procession, mechanically moved aside for her to pass, closed again, and hid her from view. The others marched on quietly.

Girls passed with flowers. Men came with revolutionary banners, white lettering on a red background: "Hail to the New Republic for which our comrades have died."

"Peace to the victims of Civil War."

"God bless those who fell for Liberty."

The rain began to fall in a blinding drizzle, but they did not seem to heed it and passed on silently.

After the banner-bearers came men and women carrying the white deal lids of the coffins, and followed by a miscellaneous crowd of young girls. Behind them a priest walked, with bent head, swinging a censer. Then, before one had time to realize that the corpses would be exposed, bare-headed men carried on their shoulders the coffins open—with the dead bodies inside. The shock robbed me completely of the power to move, and I remained frozen with horror.

There were heads severed from bodies, limbless trunks, crushed faces, green, black, grey, and a startling white, hair matted with blood. One body was covered with a piece of white muslin, but as it passed a puff of wind caught the shroud in the air and revealed a black, contorted face and a trunk in pieces. And all the while there was the sickening odour of putrefaction. A voice at my side roused me and I ran away, out of sight of the coffins (which passed for three hours) and far from the sound of tramping feet.

This was the only demonstration which the Ataman permitted. The Don district was declared an independent republic, and ministers were chosen. Meetings likely to prove disorderly were, for the time being, forbidden, and anything which tended to stir up strife was sternly repressed. The streets looked different, and although beggars still abounded, there seemed to be fewer soldiers of the hooligan type. The carriages of the bourgeoisie once more clattered over the cobbled streets and well-dressed girls and boys sauntered up and down the Sadovaya.

There were several other good streets, but they never seemed to walk anywhere else, and sometimes during the fashionable hours, between twelve and two in the afternoon, the Sadovaya was so crowded that it was almost impossible to move, and unless one stepped off the pavement and walked along the road one had to be content with standing in a queue and moving only when the person in front allowed this privilege. As the old peasant woman predicted, the "bourguikas" were no longer afraid to wear hats, and now that the Cossacks were in power no one hesitated to show that she had boots at five hundred roubles a pair and a "shooba" at five thousand.

Attempts were made to cope with the brigandage, which had increased to an alarming extent during the months before the battle, and the Cossacks who guarded the streets shot at robbers or arrested them. Their efforts improved the situation slightly, though at one time it seemed as though two new thieves took the place of each one that was killed or imprisoned. Our house was so near the steppes that ne'er-do-wells haunted the street, and we were often awakened by the Cossacks' rifle shots and the shouts of pursuers and pursued. One night some keys were found in a small hole by our back gate. The night watchman saw them glittering in the lamplight, picked them up, and put them in his pocket just as a girl came to him and begged him to go to the street corner and help reorganize the queue outside the bakery, which had become disorderly. He went with her, and returned in ten minutes to find five men wandering about in front of the house, evidently searching for something. He shot twice in the air and they ran off.

The next morning the keys were found to fit our front and back doors and the garden gate, so that we knew we had a traitor in the house. Mme. Sabarova became very nervous, and always went round the house at night, trying all the doors to see if they were properly locked. She made a servant sleep in each of the sitting-rooms, on the sofas, so that every room should have an occupant. The dvornik was installed on a horse-hair couch in the greenhouse, and when I passed through at night I used to find him lying like Bottom in the fairy wood, surrounded by leafy shrubs and green palms.

I do not think he would have been much use in the case of a burglary, as we all used to pass in and out while he was sleeping and he never turned a hair. The only advantage of his presence there was, that when once definitely awake he would not have to waste time dressing, as he always slept in all his clothes, plus an ancient and mangy fur cap and long felt boots. He kept a spade at his side. I never knew why, and when I asked him he only answered enigmatically, "It is good for many things."

Mme. Sabarova did not seem to have much faith in her household guardians, and her anxiety reached such a point that before going to bed she used to look underneath the tables and feel behind the clothes in the cupboards lest a thief should be hiding there. I once asked her laughingly what she would do if she found one, but she was so upset at my joking about it that I never dared mention the subject again. In spite of her fears she went to the theatre two or three times a week, dressed in costly furs and with emeralds the size of thrushs' eggs in her ears, and, though I often suggested that it was unsafe, she allowed Natasha to go out for walks wearing pearl and diamond earrings and a pearl necklace. She maintained that the thieves would not know the value of a pearl. This may have been true, but every one in Rostov knew Natasha Sabarova, and knew also that she was one of the richest girls in the town and might easily be wearing valuable jewels.

The rich bourgeoisie were not in the habit of hiding their wealth under a bushel, and so, although we were always escorted by an armed man, who sat on the box with the coachman, these bi-weekly visits to the theatre were a source of great anxiety to me. On one occasion we reached the corner of the main street at eleven o'clock, when the coachman suddenly turned the horses and galloped in another direction. Our gendarme was quite unconcerned.

"There are one or two corpses in the road," he explained.

Natasha smiled. "It is only thieves," she said composedly, powdering her nose. "I am glad the Cossacks kill them so that we can be comfortable and gay. Is my nose very red, Little Spider, dear?"

Christmas came and passed. We had a tree and a family party, but there were very few festivities. Christmas trees were scarce and expensive, and the prices of food had again risen. Few people were in the mood for gaiety since bad news was received daily from the "Russian Front," as the site of the fighting between Junkers and Bolsheviks was then called. The European War was rarely mentioned. In some cases it was forgotten.

"Why don't the English come and help us?" said Mme. Sabarova to me times out of number. "If they could break through the Dardanelles, sail up the Black Sea, and land four thousand men in Odessa," etc., etc., and so the Russian bourgeoisie talked, while the Dobrovolchesky (volunteer) Army of Junkers and Cadets appealed daily for recruits, and the queues of well-dressed men outside the cinemas stretched half-way down the road.

A snow storm whitened the last hours of the old year, and we sat up till midnight, playing strange games, melting wax by the fire, hardening it in cold water, and holding the lump up to the wall to see the shadows of our lovers. A gadalka (fortune teller) came and sat in a darkened room predicting the future of each person who visited her. She was an old woman with a creased, yellow face and claw-like hands. Only her eyes seemed alive, and she sat with a little bag full of beans and pebbles, which she shook up and down, saying, as each different object dropped on to the table, that we should be rich or poor, happy or miserable.

Natasha was disappointed. "I am not to marry me till I am nineteen, so must I stay here and be borded" (bored) "for two more years."

She sighed deeply, and was quite depressed until she decided that another method might prophesy a more hopeful future. She sent for six little dishes, set them in a circle on the floor, placing in one a ring and in the others a bunch of keys, water, grain, money, and a packet of sweets. A live cock was then brought cackling from the yard, seized by the wings, and dropped into the middle of the circle, where it thoughtfully considered the dishes and pecked at the one it liked best. If the cock pecked the ring, she who had dropped it into the circle would marry within the year; if at the water, the husband would be a drunkard; if the grain, keys, money, or sweets were touched, he would be greedy, miserly, rich, or luxurious. My experiment was attended by a quite unorthodox action on the part of the cock, which struggled till I dropped it, flapped its wings, and fled shrieking into a corner of the room. This cast a gloom over the proceedings, and every one agreed that it was a bad omen.

New Year's Day was a universal holiday, and all shops were shut. The Cossack patrols still wandered through the streets, but they did not interfere with the drunkards who rolled about, as the town was orderly in other respects and no attempt was made to hold public meetings.

As the days passed, those recruiting for the Dobrovolchesky Army doubled their efforts. The walls of theatres and cinemas were covered with posters appealing to all healthy men and women to join the Junkers and help them protect Rostov. The Cossacks were urged to remember their magnificent history and to fight for the land of their fathers. Young men of military age were begged to support their brothers and save the town from "the Hun, the Antichrist, and the Hooligan," but the Hun, the Antichrist, and the Hooligan were known to be well equipped and to have good wages, and so the appeal remained, in most cases, unanswered. The schoolboys alone seemed to show enthusiasm, and it was pitiful to see these youngsters of fifteen, sixteen, and seventeen marching through the streets in their ill-fitting uniform, while so many who were older and stronger lounged about the cinemas or spent their time at the theatres.

A small boy of twelve, who was distantly related to the Sabaroffs, came up one day dressed in khaki.

"Why, you are in uniform, Meesha," we said, amazed, and he told us with quick, nervous little gestures and shining eyes that he was one of the hundred and fifty children between the ages of eleven and fifteen who wanted to save Rostov, and so had joined the Dobrovolchesky Army as bomb-throwers. They wore uniform and were provided with three hand-grenades and a pair of wire clippers, and they were useful because they were small and not easily seen.

"When some of the boys heard the guns they were frightened and cried," said the child, "but," he added proudly, "the officers said we were men."

Towards the middle of January wounded officers were brought from Taganrog, where the fighting had been fierce, and many of the young girls helped to prepare hospitals in the big houses and canteens at the station. It was said that some of the dead bodies which were picked up were terribly mutilated. The eyes had been put out, feet hacked off, and patterns carved on the thighs. Whether these outrages had been committed before or after the death of the victim, no one knew, but very many bodies were treated in this way. A pitiful story was told me by one of the nurses, of a Junker, who would not let her leave his side, and who called out in delirium: "Sistritza, sistritza" (little sister), "kill me before they come. Don't let them beat me to death."

When the fighting drew nearer we heard the guns daily and the station was filled with young officers.

"What can we do?" said one of them to me; "we fight, fight, fight, but they are thirty to one."

"Isn't Rostov helping you?"

"Go into the Sadovaya any day and you will not ask me that question again. Rostov could do three times as much as she has done. Inertia is the curse of our country," he said bitterly. "They will give money for equipment, milk for the hospitals, because that needs no personal effort, but they won't make themselves uncomfortable. We need the money of course, but we are in greater need of men."

"What about the Cossacks?"

He shrugged his shoulders. "The history of the Cossacks is finished."

"But, Alexis Michaelovitch, that can't be true. The Don Republic is a great triumph. It will be democratic without being extreme. Kaledin has the confidence of the people."

"Wait till to-morrow's conference, mademoiselle, and then you will understand."

We waited for news of the conference, standing at the telephone the whole evening, till we received the trunk-call from Novocherkask. The message was brief but significant. Kaledin had committed suicide.

CHAPTER IX
Enter the Bolsheviks

THE DEATH OF Kaledin was a signal for great anxiety. The civilian population thought that his victory in November would inspire the Don Cossacks with confidence, and that they would rally round him when the Bolsheviks approached. Little by little, however, they began to realize that only a section of the Cossacks could be trusted, and that they must pin their faith to the Junkers. They could only hope that Rostov might be saved, but the news grew steadily worse, and the tales of the wounded officers more heart-rending, so that most people realized the fall of the town was imminent. Canteens were in full working order at the station, hospitals were prepared, but were occupied for a few weeks only, for when the hostile army drew nearer, wounded officers were moved to Novocherkask lest they should be murdered in bed by the Red Guard, who had been known to attack the sick men in the hospitals at Taganrog.

There were spies everywhere, and most people were careful not to mention the names of their friends connected with the Dobrovolchesky Army.

"How are the poor invalids?" we used to ask each other when speaking of them. If the reply was, "They are very sick," we knew that the Army had retreated still further with losses. "They are improving," meant an advance; "There is no change," that they were holding their ground. When a short advance was reported, the bourgeoisie waited with bated breath for news of a victory, but bad tidings always followed, and an atmosphere of gloom spread over the whole town.

ENTER THE BOLSHEVIKS

Towards the middle of February, Rostov was rarely free from the sound of the guns, and we used to watch the flash of the cannon across the river, while Bataisk was being bombarded, knowing that each minute brought the Bolsheviks nearer. Hope was quite dead, and people trusted that, since the town must be left to its fate, it would be abandoned before the Red Guard bombarded and destroyed it. While the Junkers were fighting like lions, but retreating step by step, some of the rich people fled to other districts. Many disguised and went to the houses of poor relations or old servants whom they thought they could trust. Money and jewels were buried in the cellars, wine hidden in the gardens. The old white or cretonne covers, used in the summer to protect the furniture from dust, were once more tied on to the chairs and sofas to hide the handsome brocade. Pictures were packed away, and many people sent their furs and best clothes in trunks to orphanages and schools which were unlikely to be searched. And while these preparations were being made, the vibration of the shots shook the windows, and as the days passed the noise seemed nearer, until on February 21st two houses in Rostov were struck by shells. The next day the sound of the firing never ceased, and we could hear the whistle of the shells as they whirred through the air.

The Sabaroffs prepared to escape. Natasha lay on the sofa threading pink ribbons into her nightdresses. The maids were too busy to help her. She lamented ceaselessly that she would have to sleep in a bed to which she was not accustomed. Her parents wandered from room to room, talking in low whispers so that the servants should not hear, and gave orders to Fräulein, who was packing a suitcase.

"Of course you do not care," they said to me one after another. "It is not your country, and the English are always cold."

IN THE STORM

I felt that I was a stranger in a strange land, and wandered aimlessly into the town. The main road looked much the same as usual, but the sleighs which were wont to stand at the corner, ready to be hired, had disappeared, and only the trams were running. A few stray carts, full of tired-looking soldiers and sacks, passed towards Nahitchovan. They looked like the vanguard of a retreating army. Everywhere one heard the remark: "Bojé moy!" (my God!), "how they're shooting." Down by the river the noise was terrific. People came out of their houses and gazed across the frozen water at the flashes in the distance. Each explosion seemed louder than the last. A crash in the adjoining street brought a crowd of boys running helter-skelter round the corner, shouting that a shell had burst. Rifle shots from the market- place drove me homewards.

The side streets were deserted. The sun was setting in a pink sky, and its gleam was reflected in the snow, making the ground look fiery. There was something indescribably desolate in the way the flakes fell, softly monotonous, while the cannon continued to boom relentlessly. In the distance some moujiks were standing by a cottage door. I walked swiftly but quietly, hoping to pass them unnoticed, but having a feeling that they would shout at me. They did.

"There goes the Sabaroffs' daughter," they cried. "just you wait, bourguika."

The breath caught in my throat and I hurried on. Each moujik I passed on the way turned and looked at me. I went so fast, and it was so slippery, that I was afraid I should fall. My brain did not seem to be working, and I kept repeating, over and over again, a quotation from Richard II:

"The pale-faced moon looks bloody on the earth,
And lean-look'd prophets whisper fearful change.
Rich men look sad and ruffians dance and leap."

ENTER THE BOLSHEVIKS

"Dance and leap - dance and leap." At last I reached the house. Natasha, who was watching for me at the window, ran out. "But you are bad. What for to go out when one shoots? I thought you were no longer in life." She looked serious. "Listen, Little Spider, you must hurry. The Dobrovolchesky Staff has gone, and we shall hide with mother and father. You will go away from here. Your English offisairs have come for you." She threw her arms suddenly round my neck. "I am glad, glad, glad. So when all is horrid you will be gay and flirt." She held me at arms' length from her, and then added whimsically, "But there, I suppose you will not. *Your Englishmen are so patriarchal.*"

At this juncture one of the patriarchs appeared and I went to pack. I do not think he has ever ceased racking his brains for the meaning of that remark.

The Sabaroffs stole out of their house at dusk. They had kept their ultimate destination a secret for fear the servants might betray them. Neither the German governess nor I knew where they had gone. Later I went with the Englishmen to a flat which they had placed under the protection of the consular seal and a notice stating that British subjects only were lodged there. We were obliged to walk, as all the isvoschiks had disappeared. It was dark. The cannon never ceased, and rifle shots seemed to be cracking all around us. We turned into the Sadovaya, where the firing was louder. The machine guns were unpleasantly near, but in spite of all this a queue of people stood before a brightly illuminated building, and I realized that the hour for the opening of the cinemas was at hand and the youth of Rostov was waiting to be amused. Will there always be a Nero to fiddle before a burning Rome?

Shortly before eight o'clock the roads were empty. None of the street lamps were burning, but a network of electric lights was arranged over the roofs of the houses, presumably for some military purpose. The trams had ceased to run, and all was quiet. For a while the snow blew in fierce blizzards and we stood watching it until supper was announced and the closed shutters hid the desolation outside. Conversation was wonderfully sustained with scarcely a pause. We depended upon one another to keep the ball rolling, but anxious eyes and pale faces belied the gay outbursts of laughter, and we were glad when the meal was over and we could sink into chairs and pretend to read.

At eleven some inspiration drew us to the window. We opened the shutter and looked out. The snow was falling quietly now. Not a soul was abroad. A shop window containing cigarettes and stationery was garishly illuminated and cast a fanlike glimmer over the white road. Suddenly a tank trundled down the Sadovaya towards the station. It moved like some great prehistoric beast in pain, and we watched it lumbering along until it was out of sight. Ten minutes later an armoured car appeared from the opposite direction. This heralded the retreat of the Dobrovolchesky Army. They came, these poor worn-out officers and soldiers, trudging wearily along the snow-covered road. They were too far off for us to see their faces, but their feet dragged, and some of them fell out of line to lean against the wall and rest for a few minutes.

Many of them were suffering from minor wounds, for their arms were in slings and their heads roughly bandaged. Their overcoats were torn, and some, who had lost their fur caps, had tied puttees round their ears to prevent frostbite. Not a sound could be heard except the distant roar of the cannon, which showed that a few Junkers had remained behind to prevent the retreating army from being followed. No one was marching briskly. Every back was bent and all eyes fixed as it were on some distant and unattainable beacon. Those who were not carrying guns supported men who were almost too worn-out to continue. Stretchers were few and far between, but sometimes a muffled burden was carried past, and occasionally a cart containing four or five recumbent glided over the snow.

Before the stragglers arrived we counted about five hundred men. Were there only five hundred against that big army of the Red Guards? One man, who came far behind the others, stood still at the corner of the street, gazing towards the station and looking up at the shuttered houses. He stretched out his arms a little and then let them fall to his sides with a quick gesture of renunciation, and after a few minutes buried his chin into his high fur collar and strode on. I could not see his face, but I knew that his eyes were fiercely sad. Why had he stood alone when the others were so far ahead? Was it to breathe good-bye to Rostov, to the town which might have done so much more, or to drop a tear for the Cossacks who had smiled while all that their forefathers had cherished crumbled away? As he turned the corner a gust of wind blew the snow round him, and he vanished in a white cloud.

We drew the curtains and went to bed. It was past midnight; the fires in the stoves had gone out and the room was cold.

For two hours I slept restlessly, until I was awakened by the cannon and a voice at my door whispering: "Get up and put something on. They're signalling over the hill."

It was one of the English girls who had been unable to sleep, and who had wandered round the house trying to find some one equally wakeful. We stood together at the window. I remember how her pretty red hair glowed against the white casement and how she nervously plaited and unplaited it as we peered into the street. From the house opposite a Red Cross nurse stole, looked up the road, then silently closed the door and walked with quick, firm steps down to the station. The cigarette shop was still illuminated.

Beyond the houses, distant gleams, preceding the noise

of the cannon, lit up the sky. On the hill some distance away flashes came and went. There was a sudden glare - a roar - then every light was extinguished, and the place was left in darkness. The guns were silent. The signals had disappeared. We waited at the window. Slowly and imperceptibly grey daylight crept along the sky. The red-headed girl did not speak. She stared into the street, twisting her hair.

"Come to bed," I whispered, taking her hand. "It is dawn."

She gave a little shiver, then walked across the room, still fingering her plait. At the door she turned and looked at me, half laughing, half crying.

"Poor old Liberty," she said.

* * *

At eight o'clock the next morning the town was very quiet. The cannon had ceased firing. There were no patrols in the roads, and the shops were all closed. The bourgeoisie slept behind their shutters, but the tovarishchi walked up and down, talking eagerly. When the Ataman had been in power, the type which was now in the street had, for a while, disappeared, but now these weary-looking men came from their hiding-places, dirty, ragged, with sad eyes and coarse lips, walking up the middle of the road with their thumbs in their armpits, or standing in groups laughing and pointing at the banks. The maid who prepared our breakfast told us that the Bolsheviks were already in possession of the town, but we did not think this was accurate. We knew, from the retreat, that Rostov had been abandoned, but we had a shrewd suspicion that the conquerors would enter in the "blood and thunder" style of a melodrama.

For two hours nothing happened, and gradually the streets filled. People timidly peeped from their doors, looked up and down, then ventured out. We were among them, and a party of us strolled into the Sadovaya while the others walked towards the steppes to see whether the peasants had assembled to greet the victorious army. The "simple people," as Natasha would have called them, were talking about the bourgeoisie, and several times the names "Sarbaroff" and "Popoff" were mentioned, sometimes with a shrug and a sneer but generally vindictively.

"They'll be a bit different after this."

"Wait till we own their mills and steamers, and sit in their big rooms on velvet chairs."

"Did you hear there would be white bread, tovarish?"

"Plenty and to spare."

We wandered among them, listening and taking care not to mention the words "Bolshevik," "Cadet," and "Junker." Their chief topic of conversation was the division of the land, and although some of them seemed bloodthirsty in their aims, the greater number appeared to want land, and land only.

Everything was as normal as possible under the circumstances, and so we continued our walk in the direction of the station, hoping to have time to call on some friends, and because we were told that a machine gun had been set up near the University, and we wanted to look at this disturber of our rest, which we had heard so continuously and never seen. A little crowd in the distance did not trouble us, and we went down towards it. Suddenly it dispersed, and people scattered to right and left, as two mounted sailors dashed full-tilt up the hill, waving revolvers and shooting in the air.

Men cheered, women screamed and seized their children by the arms, the hair, or any part of their anatomy that was nearest; young girls dashed into gateways; workmen pushed one another out of the way; a small boy fell and shrieked with pain as some one trod on his hands. There was general panic, and then the machine gun began. No one knew its target.

People pushed and jostled one another, slipping on the ice in the gutters as they made for the nearest porches, and cursing those who hindered their progress.

We took cover in the house of some Russian friends, whom we found sitting with the shutters drawn as two bullets had crashed through the window. The lady of the house was in tears. Her husband had escaped the evening before, while the Dobrovolchesky Army was in retreat, and she did not know whether he was safe. He had worked energetically for the Cadet party, and now held his life in his hands. We remained here for about an hour as the firing continued for some time, and the crowd, which was welcoming the triumphant Bolsheviks, became rather unruly.

Later we went home by a side route, wandering up alleys and finally entering the bank under our flat by a back way and creeping up a spiral staircase till we reached our own kitchen. Two of the younger officers, second lieutenants, arrived simultaneously, and were greeted with shouts of laughter, for they had put old civilian topcoats over their uniform and Russian caps on their heads. They had driven into Nahitchovan to fetch one of the Englishwomen who was alone there, and, as officers' uniforms were to the tovarishchi as red rags to the bull, they had thought it better to take no risks, seeing that every man in the crowd was armed.

Shortly afterwards, the others who had ventured out earlier in the morning, and had made their way towards the steppes, returned. They had seen a section of the triumphant army enter the town, and the excitement had become so intense that they were afraid they might be recognized as the "bourgzhui" and attacked, so they hurried home. They told us how the soldiers had marched in singing and laughing, and how the men greeted them with cheers and shouts, clapping one another on the back and slapping their thighs. Some of them started that queer Russian dance, when they hop in a sort of sitting position near to the ground, kicking out their legs in front.

Thus it was with the men, but the women seemed to be completely carried away by their enthusiasm. They danced wildly, flinging their arms above their heads and falling about in the snow. They laughed and cried, kissed each other, hugged the victorious soldiers, gave and took all sorts of rough and tumble treatment. One old toothless creature unwound a yellow scarf from her head and, waving it in the air, danced and shuffled, shrieking "Hurrah!" Another was swaying in a sort of trance, chanting, "O Lord God! O my Lord God! let the rich be slain. God, God, God!" Her eyes rolled upwards and she opened and shut her hands.

"By gum," said one of the American Y.M.C.A. workers who had joined us, "I guess they'd all gawn clean daft. got into a blue funk and beat it."

Everywhere rich families were being mentioned by name, and we wondered whether we were in a dangerous position, as we were living over a bank in the main road, in a flat owned by a well-known capitalist. We had, of course, our notice on the door signed and sealed by the British Consul, but we did not think this would prevent intrusion, as most of the Red Guard were illiterate and could neither read nor write.

After dinner, which we had according to the usual South Russian custom at three o'clock, we were startled by what seemed to be a bombardment at our very door. At first we thought that a salute was being fired in honour of the Bolsheviks, and rushed to the window. In the space of a few seconds we realized what was happening. The town was being bombarded from within. Machine guns were being fired, rifle shots rang out. Women and children, shrieking, were crowded together in doorways, crushing one another against the walls.

The bodies of civilians lay bleeding in the road. We went down to the ground floor and sat on the stairs.

The street fighting must have lasted for a couple of hours. The noise was deafening, and every now and then, when the guns paused, a human voice screamed. We none of us knew the reason for this sudden outburst. Perhaps some one had been shooting at the patrols, or possibly the Red Guard wished to terrorize the inhabitants and so keep the streets clear. Our porter looked out. He told us that dead bodies were lying in pools of blood all along the road, and that many of the corpses were naked.

"They are rounding up the Cadets and Junkers," he said, "and shooting them as they find them."

All night we heard the revolver shots.

CHAPTER X
Under Bolshevik Rule

AT SIX O'CLOCK the next morning our maid stole out of the house. She was going to the market to buy bread and hoped to escape notice as the day was still young. At the corner of the street, the naked body of a fair-haired boy lay stretched across the curb in the snow. She crossed herself and covered it with her apron, but the soldiers, who stood beside it, laughed. They had sold the clothes and boots in the market and were counting the notes. Nastia hurried on. Near the church two more nude bodies lay face downwards. The blood still dripped into the gutter. A soldier, passing by, jerked his thumb over his shoulder and pointed at them.

"Cadets," he said, and spat. Then a man came with a cart, threw the bodies in and drove on. At the corner he stopped again, picked up the dead boy whom Nastia had covered, shouted "Huh!" to his horse, and jolted down the street. He was driving a cart instead of a sleigh and the snow clogged the wheels and made his progress slow, but "My passengers are not particular," he said to Nastia, as she turned in at the door. Her story made us decide to stay at home, and we settled down to await developments.

At about eleven o'clock a peremptory summons at the door disturbed our peace, and we let in six soldiers. Each carried a rifle and a revolver, and their leader, an uncouth lad of about twenty years of age, roughly demanded our firearms. They refused to believe us when we said we had none, and searched al over the flat, poking into every corner and looking under the beds. They found black bread in our larder where they expected to see cakes, and their astonishment was unbounded.

"But you are the bourgzhui," they said; "where is your white flour?"

We had none, and said so, quickly opening the bins and cupboards. We wanted to get them out of the kitchen as soon as possible, as their sheepskins smelt so strong.

Another noise at the door drew us into the passage and we opened to a second search-party. Its chief, this time, was a bright little fellow who could not have been a day more than sixteen. He stumped into the dining-room, motioning to his men who grouped themselves behind him.

"Your firearms," he said. politely.

"We have none," we answered.

He looked at his revolver and waved it about in such a casual way that we each kept one eye on it all the time he was speaking.

"We are British subjects."

"Oh!" he said, "we beg your pardon. We have no quarrel with you. Tovarishchi, give back anything you have taken. Come on."

They clattered through the hall and we watched them from the stairs. The little leader hitched his gun on his shoulder, saluted with the charming smile of a happy-go-lucky schoolboy, and disappeared into the street. We returned to find the red-headed girl, with a little wrinkle in her nose, sprinkling eau-de-Cologne on the kitchen floor.

Later in the morning one of the officers returned. He and two others had been arrested at their house but liberated by the Bolsheviks at headquarters, and he had hurried round to see how we were. Unfortunately he had brought a revolver with him, and, hearing our story of the two search parties, decided that he had better take it out of the house and, if challenged on the way, give it up and get a receipt for it as being the possession of a British subject. In the meantime he put it on his dressing-table.

A few minutes later, Nastia, who was cleaning the room, found it, and, hearing voices in the passage, fled with it to the attic, where she hid it. As she came down the stairs there was a terrific noise outside and loud, angry voices demanding an entrance. One of us opened the door, and as the tovarishchi, followed by two civilians, surged in, anger at white heat, Nastia whispered: "Don't be afraid; I've hidden the gun in the attic."

The tovarishchi shouted at us, shaking their revolvers: "You are accused of shooting at the patrols from the top window. Give us your firearms or we'll turn the machine guns on to the house."

They went up the stairs to the attic and we looked at one another, horror-stricken. The discovery of that revolver would have meant certain death for the men of our party, but fortunately the soldiers were too drunk to search properly, and they came down empty-handed, but vowing vengeance.

We watched them go out, and we sat down and waited for the machine gun, filling in the time by playing bridge. A loud report brought the game to a standstill. Two bullets crashed through the window, and we went into the passage between thick stone walls. "Polly," as we had nicknamed the machine gun, had never been so lively before. She simply stood there and tittered at us for about two hours. We walked up and down. We talked. We had a short concert. Someone began "O God, from Whom all blessings flow," but as a bullet punctuated the first line by coming through the kitchen window, the occasion did not seem appropriate, so we tried "John Brown's Body." But we could not drown the rattle of the guns, and when the noise increased we just sat on the floor and waited. The poor old cook crouched in a corner moaning, and the Colonel walked up and down, rubbing his hands and trying to reassure her by remarking cheerily: "This is a damn fine country of yours, cookie; damn fine. Eh, what?"

Of course she did not understand a word he said, and I am sure she thought us all very hard-hearted, for we were helpless with laughter.

For three days the Bolsheviks brought their machine guns into the main street, and at four o'clock fired at no special target for a couple of hours. They did little material damage beyond breaking windows and chipping plaster of the walls, but as one had no idea as to what they might do next, the whole proceeding was very nerve-wearing. Our house was in the Sadovaya, and the position was dangerous, so we decided to evacuate and go to different friends. Shortly after this the British officers left Rostov and we reluctantly bade them goodbye. They had been such a comfort to us, and we felt that no one else could have looked after us so well or treated us with such friendliness and courtesy.

* * *

As the orators had predicted, the city was "washed with blood." The Red Guard, searching systematically from house to house, arrested anyone in whose possession they found a military uniform, and killed any Junker who was hiding. Many of these boys pretended to be servants in their fathers' houses, but were denounced by the real employees and shot before their own doors. Others put on old leather coats and sheepskin hats, and disguised as tovarishchi, tried to escape by train, but slim fingers and refined features betrayed them and they were bayoneted before they reached the station. Some hid with peasants whom they thought they could trust, but were given up when the Red Guard passed the cottages.

Others fled to the cemetery and hid for days among the graves, but were driven out by hunger. Once a number of friends took refuge in a newly built tomb and remained there for three days, until one went mad and starvation forced another into going out and seeing whether he could get food. He threw himself on the protection of the porter's wife. She comforted him with gentle words, giving him soup and promising to help him, but when he was sitting in the kitchen, resting, she brought in the Red Guard, who shot him. In the meantime a lady whose daughter was buried in the cemetery visited the grave and found the Junkers. She was so touched by their misery that she went home, disguised herself as a peasant, and returned with friends dressed as workmen. They brought food and clothes, buried the Junkers' uniforms in the tomb, and wished the boys God-speed. Some of them escaped, but others were recognized and shot.

Many a young man, weary with hiding and driven from pillar to post, gave himself up and stood against the wall with head erect and shoulders thrown back, as the tovarishchi prepared to shoot.

"They are fine," said one of the soldiers, "I hate to kill them"- but "They cannot fight," said another. "They sent an armoured train down the other day. Twenty of them were in it. Twenty against all of us. That's not fighting. They were all killed, but when we came up, three nurses, who were there, stood with revolvers in each hand and blazed away without stopping. We bombed them. Of course we did not want to, but oh, well, that's not fighting."

Poor little Red Cross sisters, standing alone with the dead Junkers lying round them and firing revolvers until they were bombed. Again, "c'est magnifique mais ce n'est pas la guerre."

Sad stories were told of young officers who, in the absence of a Bolshevik official, and weary with waiting for death and listening to the insults of the Red Guard, themselves gave the order to shoot and fell with a swift sigh of relief. Children saw their parents killed. Wives begged in vain for their husbands' lives. The pathetic tale of a little Cadet made mothers realize that even the children were not safe. The father of this little boy was shot before his son, and when the soldiers came up to him the child was trembling with fear. "You can follow your cursed parent," they said as they took his arm. "Permit me to lie down," said he, "I am so weak." So they shot him as he lay on the ground.

Day after day these murders were committed. People grew almost callous, and the little street urchins laughed when they heard the shots. Once we were greeted by shouts of mirth as we turned a corner, and a crowd of small boys rushed towards us.

"Oh, barishnie," they laughed, "they've cut off the head of a Cadet. It's lying on the ground, we are trying to hit the nose with snowballs."

We rarely went out these days unless it was absolutely necessary, and then we dressed very quietly, and wore shawls round our heads like the peasants. Many a rich "bourguika," in disguise, passed us and we dared not recognize her, for the streets were full of spies and a quick smile or little nod might have done untold harm. Students whom we knew, and young officers dressed as workmen, looked at us casually as though we were complete strangers, and we passed them without a word, rejoicing one day that they had escaped and hearing the next that they had been discovered and shot.

A few notes from my diary what occurred from day to day—:

Feb. 27th. A—was here to-day. She says that early in the morning she passed the Palace Hotel, outside which there was a large pool of blood. I have not been out, but watched from the window. The streets are full of tovarishchi in old sheepskin shoobas and astrakhan caps. They are all armed, sometimes they have a rifle on their backs as well as in their hands, and each one has a revolver which he carelessly waves about as though it were a little flag. They go to the doors of the houses and beat on them with the butt ends of their rifles till they are opened, when they surge up the stairs hunting the Junkers and "requisitioning" (for purposes of the State, so they say) anything to which they happen to take a fancy. Some of them are wearing swords encased in exquisitely chiselled sheaths inlaid with Caucasian ironwork. Sometimes they carry them in their hands or at their hips, sometimes wear them slung across their backs like a rifle, but always, unused to such weapons, they are incommoded by them, always reminded of the booty they have dragged from some dead Junker.

Feb. 28th. The M-'s have suffered so much, poor things. I met Mme. M- to-day in one of the side streets. She was dressed as a servant and she looked quickly at me, half afraid, as though she thought I might recognize her, but I passed on without a sign. The soldiers came into their house, looking for the son, but luckily the boy is a general favourite among his father's workmen, who have hidden him. Mme. M- begged on her knees for her husband's life; but the soldiers pushed her away, telling her they detested screaming women. When Monsieur M- appeared they laughed at him and said they preferred his wealth to his life and that shortly he, "who had sipped, drop by drop, the blood of the people," would be a beggar in the street. And, indeed, all their property has been confiscated. Their daughter, who goes about freely without a disguise, tells me that they have only enough money to last for three weeks.

March 1st. It is said that a list of volunteers was left in the recruiting offices and that the Red Guard now knows the name of every person who helped the Dobrovolchesky Army.

March 2nd. The doctor says the Infirmary is a mortuary for slaughtered officers, and that some of the bodies have fantastic patterns carved upon them, and are minus eyes, tongues, and ears.

March 3rd. Blood, blood, blood.

March 4th. Katya's friend, who went into hiding with her brother, was arrested with him by the Red Guard. The two foolishly tried to go home and are now in prison until their father, on whose head there is a price, shall voluntarily give himself up and take their place. If the father does not appear within six days the girl and her brother are to be shot.

March 5th. M- passed through the Pushkinskaya Oolitz to-day. He was out before breakfast. On the other side of the road a student was walking. "Ha!" cried a tovarish, "another of the intelligentsia. So you will educate yourself above the people, will you? There!" And he shot him through the head. The boy fell with a little cry, and before he was quite dead his clothes were taken off and sold to a passing peasant.

March 6th. The B- 's have had all their mills, etc., confiscated and are now without resources. They seem to have disappeared. A number of soldiers are living in their house.

March 7th. M- was here again. He is trying to rescue a Junker girl who nursed in the hospital and has been imprisoned. I wish he would keep out of the streets. He walks about as if he had played no part in the great game, and if he is recognized he will be shot. He went the other day (sheer madness on his part) to the station, which he says was a perfect shambles! The officers were trying to escape by train. They disguise as workmen, but a detachment of the Red Guard examines the hands of passengers, and anyone who has delicate fingers is killed. A lot of these youngsters are working in the factories simply to coarsen their hands."

Every day has some such entry, and reading it through one wonders how life could have been bearable.

All this time I had no news of the Sabaroffs. People who had heard their names discussed in the market told me that Monsieur Sabaroff was wanted, dead or alive, and I imagined that he was no longer hiding with his wife and daughter, but in a separate place. The telephone was working and I rang up Fräulein, speaking guardedly, without mentioning names. She begged me not to come near the house, as a guard had been placed round it and she was not allowed to go beyond the garden. She had had a bad time. Part of a shell had burst in the dining-room, making a large hole in the roof, breaking the dormer windows and filling the place with dust.

Three search parties had been all over the house and the soldiers had stolen ornaments. The first set had been drunk and had kissed and flirted with her till she was speechless with fear. They went away without troubling her further, but the others who arrived shortly after abused her, using the coarsest of epithets when they addressed her and beating her with their rifles because she trembled so much that she could not open the doors quickly enough. They roared with laughter when she showed signs of fear and forced her at the point of the bayonet to prepare them a meal, which they devoured, pocketing the forks and spoons when they had finished. The third party accused her of harbouring Korniloff, and sought for him all over the house, spitting on the floors and prodding the beds and chairs with their bayonets. A number of them remained behind to guard the house. The servants had stolen the wine and spent the night dancing and singing. Some of them came to her room and told her that she must join them as every one was now equal and she was no longer a barishnia.

Mme. Sabarova's brothers, the Popoffs, in whose firm her husband was a partner, had escaped, or in any case were nowhere to be found. Had they been discovered they would certainly have lost their lives, for they were sought high and low and their name was dragged through the gutter by every tovarish. Their mills and boats were confiscated and illiterate workmen were in charge of their offices. The local Soviet wished to find them that they might, at a small salary, give advice regarding the business, which no one else knew how to conduct. But of course they did not appear. Their house was ransacked and everything of value stolen. The cook, a refined-looking girl, was thought to be her mistress in disguise and was promptly bound by the soldiers, who held pistols at her head and told her to give up her husband, if she did not wish to see her children torn limb from limb. Fortunately her fellow-servants identified her and told a coherent story, so that the Red Guards reluctantly unfastened the cords. They tried to bribe the other servants with promises of jewels to give up their employers, but the maids did not know of their whereabouts, and so the soldiers went out, but before leaving the house they cut the portraits of Monsieur and Mme. Popoff from the frames and took them away.

In the meantime the Bolsheviks had been drawing up their laws.

Their first move was to take over all the banks and to confiscate the money for the State. They gave each bankers' client a maintenance allowance of a hundred and fifty roubles a week, irrespective of the number of people whom this man had to support. So that a family of two received the same as one of seven, unless the latter contained two people banking in different places, in which case the amount would be doubled, a hundred and fifty roubles being drawn from each account. The allowance was ridiculously inadequate, as prices wore so high, and many families were on the verge of starvation.

In addition to this difficulty the rich people had to face another. Many of them had withdrawn vast sums from the banks and buried the notes in their gardens, or hidden them on their persons, as soon as they realized that Rostov would fall into the hands of the Bolsheviks. The bankers' ledgers proved this, and the Soviet taxed the bourgeoisie on the grounds that the town had resisted and must therefore pay a tribute. This tribute was twelve million roubles. Each rich inhabitant had to pay a sum proportionate to his wealth. He could not draw the money from the bank but must collect it from his friends or produce it somehow. Foreign subjects were not immune from this legislation and were obliged to pay as much as the Russians.

The Bolsheviks held that their wealth had been amassed in Russia and was therefore taxable. This law caused great consternation, particularly when three bourgeois were arrested and kept as hostages. People who had buried very little money were at their wits' end. One old lady of seventy-six was unable to pay her share and sat for days weeping in prison, whither she had been hauled. Her solicitor begged that she might remain a prisoner in his house, but the request was refused.

She had plenty of money in the bank and offered to pay twice the amount demanded if she could but take it from her account. She was told that anything she might think she possessed, beyond the maintenance allowance allotted her, was the property of the State. No one could lend her the money and so she was arrested. It took a long time to find twelve million roubles, and when at last about half the sum had come in, it was announced that the treasurer had disappeared and with him the tribute money; so they had to begin collecting all over again: and those who were not obliged to pay were amused. At the time five different forms of money were in use: the old Nikolievski money (pre-war), the Kerensky notes, coupons printed after the fall of Kerensky, the Don Republic money ordered by Kaledin, and the Don notes issued by the Bolsheviks. The people who had jewels hoped to be able to sell them, but the safes were commandeered by the Bolsheviks, and no one was allowed to take anything from the banks excepting the maintenance allowance. Those who had been prudent enough to hide their jewels could not profit by their forethought, as no one had money to spare for anything beyond the barest necessities.

The strictest economy was necessary, and when a law was passed that servants could claim a hundred roubles a month, people reduced their staffs, and the registry offices were crowded with women who could not find work and grew daily more discontented. The Menshevik organ "Rabochy Krai" was suspended for protesting that the Bolsheviks were not fulfilling their promises, and that if the workmen remained out of employment much longer, further dissension would follow. It pointed out that bread was scarcer than before. This was true. The day of their victory the Bolsheviks promised limitless white bread. The next morning this was sold in quantities. The following day the supply did not meet the demand. Afterwards black bread was sold in its place at a high price. Even that was scarce, and one day I met a crowd of peasants following a man who had a black loaf tucked under his arm.

"Tovarish, tovarish, where did you get that? Will you sell half? No? Well, at least a slice?"

"What do you take me for? This may be the last I shall get for a week."

UNDER BOLSHEVIK RULE

The Bolshevik regime had, for a short time, a bad effect upon education. Money could not be used for luxuries, and so nearly all private tuition, which is popular in Russia as a preparation for school examinations, came to an end. Lessons in music, art, and dancing were stopped, for there was nothing with which to pay the teachers. Foreign tutors suffered, and one English lady lost fifteen pupils in a week. Not only did private tuition cease but there was a movement to abolish all forms above the fourth, as many of the Bolsheviks in office were illiterate and could neither read nor write, and they considered that an education which dealt with anything beyond the barest elements of learning pandered to the needs of the intelligentsia and brought one man above his neighbour.

For weeks on end the schools closed, because parents were afraid to send their children lest they should be mistaken for the little Cadets who had helped the Junkers or for the sons of officers. Many of the masters and elder boys were in hiding; and when at last the schools reopened the Red Guard stood at the gates and arrested or shot the lads whom they suspected of having had dealings with the Dobrovolchesky Army.

"What have you done?" cried the mother of a little fellow of twelve. She had arrived at the school door just as one of the soldiers whipped out a revolver and killed her child. "He never did anything against you."

"Oh!" said the soldiers, "you must excuse us. We thought he was F-'s son"; and they went away, leaving the little bleeding body in the road.

Many of the older gymnasists did not return to school and discarded their grey uniform, sometimes going about in the black tunics and breeches worn by errand boys, so as to avoid being recognized. The "Rabochy Slov," a newspaper which had taken the place of the "Rabochy Krai," was no longer allowed to be published, as it protested in very strong language against this murder of little boys and of young officers who were scarcely more than children.

Prayers and religious instruction were omitted from the school curriculum for, at the time, there was a feeling against religion. God had been "above the people," and was therefore in the same category as the aristocrats and must be abolished. Soldiers and ruffians who were in the habit of entering houses to pillage had hitherto respected the jewelled icons, but now they tore them from the walls and packed them together with other valuables which they had stolen.

"Mother of God, Mother of God, help us!" cried one of my friends when a search party entered her house.

"Be silent," said a soldier, seizing the cross which hung round her neck. "How can there be a mother of God when there's no God? Now we have Liberty"; and he lurched over to the icon and laughed.

Since the patriarch of Moscow had issued a proclamation, urging the country to put a stop to "this fratricidal civil war," and anathematizing the Bolsheviks, the priests had become unpopular, and once a crowd of men pursued three of them, crying, "Krov! Krov!" (blood, blood). But the women, still superstitious as regards the power of these holy men, were afraid and appealed to the Soviet, outside whose gates the crowd had gathered. The soldiers were sent to protect the priests, who were accompanied home, but treated with contempt. Afterwards many of them were afraid to go outdoors, and were forbidden to take part in funeral processions, which were pathetically frequent, so that one missed these picturesque long-haired figures, whose vestments used to make such a wonderful splash of colour among the mourners of the dead.

The university suffered because several of the students had joined the Dobrovolchesky Army and left the town. One professor known to be in favour of the Cadet party was killed;

another, who had always worked for the people and tried to alleviate their burdens, was shot simply because he was one of the intelligentsia. The students, who loved the man dearly, were afraid to follow the coffins to the grave lest they, too, should be attacked; but little groups of sailors stood outside the church door and on their caps they wore white ribbons printed with the words: "Death to the Bourgeoisie."

At one time specialization came under the Bolshevik ban, and an attempt was made to introduce general lectures of a popular order instead of those given on the higher branches of the different subjects. Nothing, however, came of this, and the students working for special degrees were left unmolested.

Another difficulty with which the bourgeoisie had to contend was the fact that their houses were no longer considered their personal property. If they owned a house which was valued at a certain number of roubles, they were obliged to pay rent in proportion to its size and position, even though they had long ago bought the land and the building itself. Not only did they have to do this, but they were only allowed to keep one room for each member of the family in addition to a sitting-room and kitchen. Any extra apartments were requisitioned for the use of people who could not find lodgings, or for the Red Guard.

Efforts were made to billet students and more refined families upon the intelligentsia, but the local committee had not always time to make satisfactory arrangements, and some people suffered dreadfully, for occasionally as many as fifteen of the Red Guard were brought into their houses and lived there, choosing the rooms they wished to inhabit and wandering about the house as they pleased. They had no respect for the furniture, soiled the carpets, tore the curtains, and at night brought women from the streets into the houses, dancing and drinking till dawn so that the inhabitants were sleepless with the noise. One lady had three sailors and their families billeted upon her. They selected her bedroom and a large drawing-room in which there was a piano, removing her possessions into a small adjoining room.

"It will be gay for you," they said, "for we shall sing and play with our friends in the evenings." They were most affable and gave her a cordial invitation to join them.

Houses which belonged to people who had escaped and which were left in the care of servants, were requisitioned altogether and in many cases completely ruined. The Sabaroffs, through a friend who was on good terms with the Bolsheviks, managed to procure a paper granting them freedom from such intrusion. It was signed by the secretary, who had evidently just been taught how to write his name, for the initial letters were not written in capitals. One lady told me that the paper she received was written in German. At the time German was freely spoken in the streets, and most of the bourgeoisie looked upon this as a hopeful sign that deliverance was at hand. They only wanted order, and now that the Brest-Litovsk Peace was signed they did not seem to mind accepting help from their former enemy. If the Entente could do nothing for them they would welcome the Germans. They preferred a foreign power to the Bolsheviks. They wanted to be comfortable again.

CHAPTER XI
The Anarchists and Departure

CONDITIONS DID NOT improve, and people lived their lives from day to day making no plans, trying to forget the immediate past and not daring to think of the future. The Little Russians from Ukraine under German leadership were supposed to be marching towards Rostov, but the Bolshevik papers did not give definite information on this point, and though rumours increased daily no one could be certain as to whether this army were near or not. A clue to the situation was given when it became apparent that the Bolsheviks were gradually evacuating. Some people put this down to the unrest in Novocherkask, for shortly after the fall of Rostov the capital of the Don district had been given up by the Cossacks without a struggle. They had not understood the principles of Bolshevism and were now indignant that the land of their forefathers was being divided, and were openly rebelling. Fighting was expected, but as it was now difficult for one town to communicate with another no one knew what was actually happening. The trains were irregular and telephoning dangerous on account of spies. No one knew what to expect, and each fresh rumour produced but little surprise. People waited apathetically. "At any rate it cannot be worse," they said.

From one point of view, however, it was worse. With the gradual evacuation of the Bolsheviks, the execution of Junkers and other enemies of the Soviet decreased, but wholesale robbery and brigandage became more frequent. It must be said in justice to the Bolsheviks that they tried to establish order and did not authorize the pillaging which so terrorized the inhabitants of the town. But attached to the Red Guard there was a large number of hooligans, who, attracted by the wages and the lack of supervision, had "joined up" simply for the sake of earning and of having an opportunity to loot. Parties of them used to go into shops and annex anything which they happened to like.

"We requisition this in the name of the State," they would say, holding revolvers to the heads of the unfortunate salesmen, who were afraid to resist.

People in private houses were treated in the same way, although the Bolsheviks shot convicted thieves and promised help to anyone who would telephone to headquarters. They failed to realize the impossibility of profiting by such aid when one was lying on the floor, bound hand and foot, or when a brigand was threatening one with a revolver. Night attacks in the streets were frequent, and the local Soviet attempted to cope with the situation by refusing to allow anyone to be out of doors after nine o'clock. One day a body was found at the corner of our road with a paper pinned to its coat: "This person was out after prohibited hours." This law, however, did not prevent houses from being attacked, as the brigands were always in the uniform of the Red Guard and held forged passports, so that those responsible for keeping order in the streets thought they were members of an official search-party and left them unmolested.

One morning when most of the Bolsheviks had retired, leaving their representatives at headquarters, we were awakened at three o'clock by the sounds of firing and the explosions of bombs. We sat up and blinked for a few minutes, then turned over and went to sleep. Familiarity breeds contempt. At breakfast some one announced dispassionately that the

THE ANARCHISTS AND DEPARTURE

Anarchists were in power. The remark elicited no comment.

In spite of their crimes these Anarchists were rather amusing. They were like children playing at brigands with real fire-arms. They dashed through the streets in motor-lorries, waving their arms and shooting in the air. They wore black crape tied round their right sleeves, just above the elbow, and black ribbons in their caps. As they motored at top speed they threw out proclamations and white leaflets, which fluttered into the gardens, caught in the branches of the trees, and were eagerly snatched by the tovarishchi walking in the town. These leaflets began with the words "Order above All," and went on to say that the bourgzhui were responsible for the disorder, as they had wealth locked in coffers in their cellars, and that if these coffers were open to all there would be no disorder. They said that liberty was at stake. People stood in the streets with expressionless faces and watched their mad career through the town.

They broke into houses in the approved cinema style, bound all the inmates but one with cords, and forced the free person at the point of the bayonet to give up anything of value in the house. Any show of resistance was answered by violence, and people were sometimes beaten black and blue with the butt end of rifles. They were clever at finding the hiding-places of valuables, and even peeled off pieces of wall-paper which were torn, to see whether rings were concealed between the plaster and covering. They had a contempt for feminine modesty and thrust their hands into the bosoms of women's clothes in case a little bag of money should be hidden there. Sometimes they forced girls to undress that they might see whether jewels were sewn into their corsets. They ransacked every room, rummaging among paper, shaking books lest rouble notes should be placed in the leaves, and even raking over the cinders. They took furniture, and it became quite a common thing to see motor lorries driven by armed sailors and filled with carpets, bicycles, bedding, and chairs which had been stolen. Household linen was much in demand, and many people packed their best things in cases and hid them in outhouses or put them in the cellar under the coal.

One family of girls living with their grandmother was attacked by a number of brigands, who forced them all to lie on their faces on the floor while five men searched the house for valuables. The remainder stood over the girls with bayonets touching their backs so that they dared not move. In the interval, the poor old grandmother fainted. The brigands were indignant at the want of filial feeling shown by the girls, who remained lying on their faces.

"How can you stay there," said one, "while the babooshka is fainting? Get up and fetch the smelling salts and water."

He prodded the nearest recumbent figure with his bayonet. The smelling salts were fetched. The tovarish revived babooshka, and when she was quite restored gently unfastened her earrings and brooch. When they had all collected what they wanted, he turned to the girls, who were still face downwards on the floor and, pointing at babooshka who was on the verge of another faint, "Vam ne stidno?" (Aren't you ashamed?), he asked.

At this time the servants could not be trusted. Many of them had friends among the thieves, and so had no scruples about leaving doors unlocked, and as the Bolsheviks had made the employment of watchmen unlawful, the houses were not protected. People in different parts of the town formed house committees, and two members of each family were on guard night and day at the front and back doors. Every four hours they were relieved. By this means the household knew who was trying to gain admittance, and let in no one who could not give satisfaction as regards his identity. Many houses had passwords.

THE ANARCHISTS AND DEPARTURE

Prices continued to be very high, as the value of the rouble was so low and transport so disorganized that nothing could be brought into the town. Material cost at least seventy roubles an arsheen, and was very inferior in quality. Mending wool and cotton were so expensive that servants could not afford to patch their worn-out clothes unless they happened to have odd bits of stuff in their possession or stole from their employers. Ready-made garments were rarely to be found in the shops, and people had no idea how they were going to dress themselves in the summer or following winter. Underlinen was exorbitant in price and materials for making it unprocurable.

The lack of material and clothes produced an increase in highway robbery, and women out at night were sometimes stripped of all that they were wearing and sent home naked. If the brigands were sympathetically inclined they gave their victim a newspaper and called a cab, saying: "Go home or you will catch cold"; but more often they got into the cab themselves and left the lady to return as best she could. In consequence, people feared to venture into unfrequented streets after dark, and many hesitated before walking in the main road at night.

Drunkenness increased, and inert masses of humanity lolled about the streets. A supply of vodka had become available at Novocherkask, and women gained money so easily that they gave up their usual work and confined their attention to profiteering in vodka, which they bought for five roubles a bottle and sold in Rostov for thirty. One taste of spirit produced an insatiable thirst, and anything alcoholic was imbibed with gusto. A friend of mine, who was discovered in his bedroom when the brigands entered, was told to get them something to drink. He produced a small bottle of liqueur. They finished it between them, but complained that it was poor stuff and that they wanted something less sweet. They wandered round the room and, finding on his dressing-table some green liquid in a bottle, consumed it with alacrity, smacking their lips and saying, "Ah, that's good! It burns." It was my friend's hair-tonic!

Anti-bourgeois processions were very frequent. They were led by soldiers and the rear brought up by armoured cars, and if we happened to pass them on a day when an east wind had blown away discretion and forced us to wear furs, we fled up an alley. The people who were marching carried red banners printed in white with the words, "Smert bourgzhui" (Death to the bourgeoisie), and they sang a Russian song of Liberty, set to the "Marseillaise," and every now and then a soldier raised his gun and shot into the air. The sight was picturesque, because all the women wore bright scarves round their heads and the men had red handkerchiefs tied to their arms, but the general public naturally disliked such demonstrations, and when five processions took place in one week we grew thoroughly ill-tempered with anxiety.

Some one started the rumour that a "St. Bartholomew's Night" was about to take place. Belief in the idea increased daily, and one week when the processions had been frequent and the articles in the papers particularly blood-thirsty, many people slept in their clothes and hid ladders under the shrubbery in their gardens so that they might escape over the wall if assassins entered their houses. But though we lived in perpetual dread, this general massacre was never more than a threat.

The Sabaroffs did not return to their house, but remained incognito with friends in another part of the town. They went about more freely now, although they stayed indoors during the St. Bartholomew scare. Their house was left in the care of the German governess and a porter from one of their mills, a fat man whose eyes disappeared when he laughed and who was lame in the left leg. He professed great devotion to the family, but afterwards dug up all the money which the Sabaroffs had buried and gave it to his wife. We did not discover this till later.

He and Fräulein were a strange couple. They had their meals together in the drawing-room, as the dining room had been destroyed by a shell, and were waited upon by a Ukranian maid called Akulina, the only servant left. All the others had been dismissed, but Akulina was so stupid that no one feared her. In the old days, when we were living at home, she was a source of great amusement to Natasha and me. She was tall and enormously fat, with very pink cheeks and a wisp of flaxen hair. She wore a tight grey blouse, too short in the sleeve, so that the cuffs were left unfastened in order to accommodate her big arms. Her skirt was of black serge, split from the knee to the hip, showing a strip of pink flannelette nether garments. Her brown stockings were full of holes, and when she walked they descended over her ankles, so that she usually arrived in one's room bare-legged or shuffling along with her fat hands firmly grabbing the stockings above the knee. We always knew when she was coming as she breathed so heavily, and we managed to contain our laughter till she was gone. If she heard a giggle she used to return and stare at us solemnly without uttering a word.

"You are so graceful, Akulina," said Natasha one day. She did not answer, but a slow grin spread over her face and she shook an admonitory forefinger three times with great deliberation.

At this point the parrot called out, "Dobry viecher, krasavitza" (Good evening, my beauty). Akulina looked all round the room with her mouth open.

"Ha, ha, ha!" said the parrot.

She suddenly became aware of the bird and stared at it. It

put its little green head on one side and cocked one eye.

"Popachka chaioo hochet" (Polly wants some tea), it said.

Akulina dropped her stockings, crossed herself devoutly, and murmuring, "The Lord save me from devils," stumped off to the kitchen as fast as her fat legs could carry her. She never passed that parrot without a sidelong glance of fear and a hasty prayer. She believed very strongly in devils and shared our fear of the Anarchists, who, she maintained, would be certain to steal her savings and her stockings, of which she was very proud. On this account she borrowed a shoe-bag from me and stuffed her treasures into it, concealing it in the bosom of her dress so that her figure looked even more odd than her Maker had intended it to be. This gift won for me her affection, and she always kissed my hands and tried to do little kindnesses for me, until we fell out on the subject of my comb, with which I found she was in the habit of disentangling the fringe of my doormat every morning.

Akulina's fear of the Anarchists was by no means unwarranted. They did not confine their attentions to the upper classes only, but robbed people in very poor circumstances who happened to be unprotected at the moment. A floor-polisher who used to be employed by the Sabaroffs was stopped in the street and relieved of his watch and a few roubles which he had earned. There were tears in his eyes when he told me of this. It was difficult for him to earn money since the eclipse of the bourgeoisie, because few people could afford to have floors polished. In the old days these men used to visit the big houses once a week. They had no brush, neither did they crawl on their knees, rubbing like a housemaid, but they were barelegged, and attached to one foot they had a wooden polisher padded with a cloth, and they walked up and down pushing this vigorously backwards, forwards, and sideways with steps not unlike those of the

THE ANARCHISTS AND DEPARTURE

Tango. They earned very little for this work, so that if they were robbed the loss was great.

The manicurist who used to visit Natasha was also attacked one afternoon. She was afterwards found in a fainting condition, gagged and bound. Not a garment was left in the house, all the food had been taken, and the best furniture was also missing. As manicuring had become a luxury she was not in a position to replace what she had lost, and could not go out on a cold day because she had no warm coat.

All this time I had been making inquiries at the Consulate regarding the approach of the Germans, and when I heard that their army was not far off, I was determined to leave Rostov. The Consul thought that it might be possible to collect a party and to arrange for a special train, in spite of the fact that the railway was so disorganized. He thought that other foreign subjects from different towns in South Russia might pass through Rostov, and he promised to let me know.

During their enforced exile I used to visit the Sabaroffs daily, taking care not to go into the house if there was anyone in the street because people knew that I was their "Anglichanka" and they did not wish their hiding-place discovered. Towards the beginning of April they became much more cheerful, as the Cossacks in Novocherkask were arming against the Bolsheviks and the Germans were definitely known to be near Tangarog.

"Only think," said Natasha, " those Anarchists, pigs and gooses that they are, have taken our box in the theatre. When the Germans come all will be in order."

"If the Germans come I shall have to go away," I said.

"Pooh, Little Spider, what for to go away? The journey will kill you. All will be comfortable when the Germans make order."

"Doubtless, but I do not want to meet the Germans. They

may keep me here for the duration of the war. I think I must go, Natasha. You shall visit me in England."

"Then you must marry you and have the ménage. And, please, Little Spider, you are so thin that you must choose a fat husband but - but not so fat as Akulina, for otherwise will your children nevair be proportioned."

She wept copiously when I finally said goodbye, hugging me in her arms and fastening a beautiful Caucasian bracelet on to my wrist. Her mother shook hands with me.

"You leave us without a regret ?" she asked. "But yes. I know. Ah, the cold English!"

Cold England seemed very far away when I was making preparations for the journey. I had two days in which to do everything, and sufficient food for three weeks had to be bought. The shops were nearly empty, as the merchants, fearing the Anarchists would steal everything, had hidden most of their durable provisions and only showed perishable goods. One other Englishwoman decided to leave Russia. She was a charming, blue-eyed creature with an almost extravagant sense of humour, a quality which is indispensable for a refugee. We called her Mamasha (little mother), because she had a comfortable way of looking after people without worrying them. She and I spent two days shopping before the refugee train arrived. Prices were appalling, and we could get nothing that we wanted. Coffee was thirty-six roubles a pound and sugar non-existent, but we managed to find some good cheese and smoked sausage, and we bought numberless eggs for hard-boiling.

The night before our departure we hardly slept at all. The Anarchists were bombarding a house where some sailors, who had offended them, were living, and the noise disturbed every one. The next morning we set off with as little luggage as possible, driving through the back streets towards the station. We avoided the Sadovaya, as we heard occasional rifle shots from that direction and feared our provisions might be "requisitioned for the State" if we were seen. Mamasha had black circles under her eyes, and I felt cold. We looked at each other and laughed in a helpless way for no reason.

"We shall never get there," she said.

"Yes, we shall," I answered, without conviction. My heart was in my boots.

We had some difficulty in discovering the train as the station was so crowded and it was impossible to leave the luggage unguarded. Soldiers of the Red Guard stood outside the gates and laughed as they pointed out the foreign bourguikas running away. Little Mamasha, with a bold face but a faint heart, valiantly shouldered her packages and staggered through the crowd to the accompaniment of jeers. I followed with a small boy and a dvornik, who took the place of porters. After wandering along the lines among numberless wagons and engines, we succeeded in finding the refugee train, which had such a fixed and stationary look that we thought we should never get off. It was surrounded by tovarishchi smoking tobacco, and Armenian beggars sitting with babies in their arms on the dusty platforms. Old wizened women, clutching baskets and puffing at dirty clay pipes, crouched against the wall staring at us. None of them spoke, and there was something indescribably depressing about this silent crowd of sad-eyed women, who simply looked at us without a word.

The refugee carriage had come from Mariupol and contained about thirty people, English, Belgian, and French. Mamasha and I climbed in and took our seats. We remained for twelve hours in the train. Our friends and pupils came to say goodbye. They wished us "good luck," but studiously avoided talking of the journey, for they all thought that we had jumped from the frying pan into the fire. The interminable waiting exhausted us before we had started, and only when we had begun to lose all hope and had discovered that the sausage which was to form our most staple means of subsistence was almost inedible, our carriage was attached to the Moscow train and the tovarishchi began to climb on to the roofs and storm the other compartments.

We were protected, as our carriage was labelled "English Mission," and was supposed to be for an official party, but in spite of this we shut all the windows lest the soldiers should try to invade us. The train was both filled and covered. Peasant women and soldiers sat on the roofs, clinging to the ventilators. Workmen got astride the buffers. Boys sat on the steps. They shouted and pushed till the whistle blew and the train slowly steamed out of the station. And the last glimpse I had of Rostov was the dusty platform crowded with soldiers and motionless beggar-women, and in the midst of them the slim blue-clad figure of the red-headed girl, standing and waving her handkerchief, while dust-coloured Armenian babies tumbled over her feet.

CHAPTER XII
From Rostov to the Murman Coast

THOUGH WE EXPECTED to be at least three weeks on the way, we were very much disappointed when the train after rolling on for about half an hour, suddenly came to a standstill and remained stationary for four hours. We prepared a meal, but the sausage was unpleasant and the coffee tasted of the tin in which it had been boiled. Everything was covered with smuts and from the far corner of the upper berth two flat red insects crawled stealthily over the cushions. The linen covering on the seats was stained, and the air smelt bad.

Mamasha looked at me. "What's the matter?" she asked, and her blue eyes twinkled.

"I feel so vilely dirty," I said irritably.

"A wash?" suggested Mamasha tentatively.

I went to the lavatory, where I made the depressing discovery that there was no water on the train, and returned, announcing the fact gloomily. The Frenchwomen who shared the coupé with us were horrified. They both began to talk at once, gesticulating and shrugging their shoulders. I heard a ripple of laughter from Mamasha's corner and looked at her. She was humming "We won't go home till morning," and polishing her face with cotton wool dipped in eau-de-Cologne.

After a while the train moved on again, and we continued our journey until just outside Novocherkask. Here we pulled up with a jerk, and the familiar sound of rifle shots greeted our ears. The tovarishchi on the roof began to shout, some peasant women screamed, the firing redoubled, and we heard what was suspiciously like a machine gun. Blowing out the candles, we pressed against the windows, listening. For some minutes we thought the train had been held up by brigands, but we gradually distinguished through the gloom the forms of soldiers, Red Guards in flight before the Cossacks. They were ducking and stumbling through underbrush, wet with melting snow, throwing down their guns as they ran. Their cries of fright, and in many cases of pain, were unspeakably harrowing, and we turned away, wondering what the daylight held in store for us. Later, some of us slept a little, crowded in together, while others remained in the corridors on sentry duty.

The next morning we found ourselves in Novocherkask. "What has happened?" we asked the soldiers, and were told that the Bolsheviks had fled in all directions. Desultory firing still continued, and the station was full of stir and bustle. Cossacks, mounted and on foot, were patrolling the town. Some were guarding the entrance to the station with fixed bayonets; others were marshalling their prisoners. The restaurant was crowded with armed men - eating, talking, laughing, and singing. Spent cartridges were on the ground, bullet-holes were in the walls, and some of the windows were broken. There was a spurious air of gaiety, but all the time one felt the under-current of anxiety forcing and forcing itself upwards. What of the morrow? Triumph for the Cossacks used not to be short-lived. But now? Well, they had thrown away what their forefathers had held as sacred; they had betrayed their town to the enemy, and, even though they had now retaken it, the knowledge of their loss was still bitter, and the hope to regain all that they had spurned but faint.

We wished to continue our journey, but as the lines had been cut both between Novocherkask and Rostov and between Novorcherkask and Voronej, we could neither go forward nor back. More fighting was expected round the station, and further delay was necessary, as the Cossacks were now in power, and official permission to leave the town had to be obtained from them. The ladies of the party were offered hospitality by some Cossack families while the men remained in the train, guarding the carriages.

Fighting continued for three days in the village behind Novocherkask; and Guluboff, who had in the March campaign persuaded the Cossacks to surrender to the Bolsheviks, was dead, killed by his own men. Cossack officers, imprisoned and under sentence of death, were liberated; but the rejoicing was subdued, for rumour was busy, and it was generally thought that reinforcements were arriving for the Bolsheviks from Rostov. One night the firing seemed nearer, and three bombs exploded in the town. The next day all was very quiet. A sort of hopeless resignation was stamped on every face, and it was whispered that the Cossacks had no ammunition.

From the big houses forlorn figures, no longer in uniform but disguised as peasants, crept out, with knapsacks of food on their backs and with eyes looking wearily across the steppes. Cossack officers and Cadets, after their three days' triumph, were going into hiding. That night we helped the family with whom we were staying to bury jewels and silver in flower-pots, to hide military buttons and epaulettes, and to destroy al traces of the Colonel, who had escaped earlier in the day. We slept without undressing, ready to spring up at a moment's notice.

At 7.30 the next morning we were startled by a banging at the door and the all too familiar summons, "Open to the Red Guard." We let in a party of ten soldiers, who advanced, each with a gun in one hand and a revolver in the other. On such occasions they were always so cumbered with arms that one almost mechanically looked for swords at their hips and daggers in their boots. We intimated that we were foreign subjects, and they apologized and withdrew without even asking any leading questions. Delighted to have brought some measure of safety to the household which had shown us so much hospitality, we sat down to breakfast.

Hardly had we begun when there was another onslaught on the door. This time our visitors were drunk. They began by eating our breakfast and pocketing our apples. They refused to look at our passports. They pushed and jostled us, demanded money, and shook their revolvers in our faces. The crippled brother of the Colonel, who owned the house, stood by his sister's chair, pale but perfectly self-possessed. She sat with a little piece of paper in her hand, mechanically tearing it into strips, her eyes fixed upon the ground. And all the time the soldiers stood over her, demanding the master of the house and threatening her with death.

To each question the cripple replied, "She knows nothing."

One of the tovarishchi sat at the desk, his sheepskin hat at the back of his head, his legs wide apart, the heels on the ground and the toes sticking up, rummaging and tearing papers he could not read and cursing because he found no money.

During this scene we received a telephone message that our train would leave the station within an hour. It caused us infinite pain to abandon this unfortunate family, but we could follow no other course.

"Tovarish," I said to one of the soldiers, "I must go out and get a cab."

He had his head almost on my shoulder, and was trying to make love to me.

"You can do what you like, little pigeon," he replied affectionately, and I ran to the door. When once outside, however, it was not so easy for me to do as I liked. There were soldiers on the pavement and they surrounded me.

"What do you mean by coming out of the house? We shall kill you. Show your papers." They advanced upon me with their bayonets.

"Now look here, little doves," I said as boldly as I could, "you can't go killing British subjects like that. It's not done." They looked quite unconvinced. "I am rather important," I said loftily. " There will be a row with the British Government if I do not arrive home safely."

They seemed impressed. "Let the barishnia go," said one, and so I escaped to find my cab. After a vain search I returned to the house, where a number of soldiers were standing round the door refusing to allow anyone to proceed to the station. Argument was useless, and if it had not been for a Danish doctor, one of our fellow-travellers, who knew Russian sufficiently well to bluff, we should never have reached the train in safety. Most of the soldiers were drunk and their tempers had begun to get nasty.

The station was filled with members of the Red Guard, and there were traces of blood in the sand. Three Bolshevik nurses wandered arm in arm along the platform flirting with the sentries. They were dirty and they did not wear uniform, but had red cross handkerchiefs tied round their sleeves. They were girls of the peasant class, and their appearance was unhygienic in the extreme. I was glad to get away from them into the train. Here the men who had remained on guard told us that the scene had been appalling. The Red Guards and their camp followers, dancing among the dead bodies of the Cossacks, had sung and drunk the whole night, and in the morning they had shot the Ataman.

Our train was as we had left it except that one window had been broken. We got into our carriage, hoping to leave the stricken city within a few minutes, but we were bitterly disappointed. For an hour we waited, listening to the shooting, which was not far off, as a battle was in progress in a village just behind Novocherkask. Later we were shunted near a little wooden shed, and an armoured train drew up beside us. There was a slight pause. Then a machine gun sounded close at hand, a six-inch cannon boomed, and the Bolsheviks began their bombardment. The noise was terrific, and had we wished to speak we could not have heard one another. But we were silent. Each of us knew that if the Cossacks replied we should be blown to bits.

The Cossacks, however, had no ammunition, and they fired only once, putting the armoured train out of action. For seven hours the Bolsheviks shelled the hamlets; for seven hours we heard the roar of the big cannon and the maddening titter of the machine gun, laughing at us from the background; for seven hours we watched the village burn. Darkness fell, and we could not light our candles. The glass from the shed window smashed round us.

Suddenly there was a shriek near at hand, followed by a sound like the howling of a mob. One of the French girls in our carriage cried, "They are coming," and fainted. We had to grope for her in the darkness, chafe her hands and give her brandy—and in the midst of all this turmoil the guns ceased firing, and the train slowly jerked its way out of the station. Shortly afterwards the shelling began again, and for a long while we could see the fires in the villages.

We travelled for several hours without stopping, still hoping we should reach Veronej before the Germans; but at this time the Russian railway system was so disorganized that we were continually halting at wayside stations, sometimes for six hours at a stretch. At one little place a Polish officer—young, well-built, in uniform but without his epaulettes got out of his carriage to exercise. He was promptly surrounded by tovarishchi, who insisted that he was a Cadet escaping from Novocherkask. This was denied by those in the train with him, but they were not believed. Proudly erect, but with white lips, he showed his papers, while the soldiers shook their fists in his face and shouted at him. He was eventually allowed to return to his seat, but the scene left an unpleasant impression and we were ill at ease.

We passed through uninteresting steppe country, where hardly a field was ploughed and where no grain was being sown, with perpetual delays so wearisome in their frequency that we were obliged to organize team races along the lines. Indeed, the train travelled so slowly and stopped so often that a peasant, who at one point had fallen off the roof, was loudly cheered two stations further along when he sauntered up and took his place.

Wild dashes for kipitok (boiled water) also did much to relieve the monotony. In Russia, at every station there is a wooden hut where boiling water can be drawn, for the Russian cannot do without his tea and travels everywhere with a kettle. As there was no water on the train, we filled every available vessel, and it was amusing to see men and women in all stages of dress and undress (sometimes we had to turn out at five o'clock in the morning) rushing with kettles, teapots, bottles, tin mugs - in fact, any sort of utensil that did not leak too badly - to get a place in the kipitok queue. Afterwards acrobatic feats were performed in the way of bathing in saucepans, and the morning greeting always took the form of "Hallo! have you washed?" Later, when we were sleeping on planks, it was "Hallo! how are your bones?" but that, as Mr. Kipling says, is another story.

Beyond Liski we continued to travel for twenty minutes at a stretch and to be stationary for about three hours, waiting for other trains which always arrived very much after they were expected and which were crowded both inside and out. At one stopping-place some of our party were greeted by a friend whom they all but failed to recognize. It was Prince T, whose estates had been confiscated and who was journeying south, disguised as a tovarish. He made an excellent hooligan with his old sheepskin coat, unshaved face, and dirty hands, and he seemed quite cheerful though he was travelling under difficult conditions in a cattle wagon, herded with peasant men and women, packed like herrings in a box.

Up to the present we had been able to get a certain amount of bread and any quantity of milk at the wayside stations. A little butter could sometimes be found, and occasionally peasant girls brought baskets of hard-boiled eggs. Milk was fairly cheap, but bread was usually about seven roubles a small loaf, and the further north we journeyed the scarcer it became, until, at Goludveena, starving children ran along the platform, holding up their hands to the passengers and begging for crusts.

On the twelfth evening we reached Moscow, where we remained for three days and revelled in hot baths. Most of us slept on the train, as accommodation in the town was both difficult to find and expensive, exclusive of meals, which cost a small fortune. We could buy no bread at all and so had to economize with what we had, which was black and composed of bits of straw and sand, in addition to rye flour so badly baked that it was glutinous and unpalatable. When we had concluded all arrangements with the Consul and had obtained permission from the Bolsheviks to leave the country, our carriage was attached to several others hired by the French and filled with officers and soldiers and a few civilian refugees who had come from different parts of Russia. From them we received the utmost consideration and were treated all the way with great courtesy. They fed us with sardines and biscuits and occasional tins of "singe," the poilus' term for "bully-beef," which were very welcome after our everlasting though not over-fresh sausage.

As the only dangers would now be due to natural causes or to the state of the Moscow to Murman railway, which is built over a frozen marsh and which sinks in the spring when the snow melts, and as there was no longer any fear of our being cut off by the Germans, we became wildly hilarious. We gave nightly concerts. We nicknamed the compartments according to the characteristics of the inmates. There was the "Consulate," where all the officials were lodged; the "Nursery" where children and flappers indulged in an orgy of sugarless tea-drinking; the "Harem," where French and English women were so closely packed that the corridor was often used as an annexe, and where the washing, hanging on slack boards, flapped in the faces of unwary visitors; the "Kitchen," where the perpetual odour of onions, acquired by bribery and corruption, permeated even the suit-cases stacked at the end of the passage.

The further north we went the colder it grew, and at every stopping-place we got out and ran races or danced to keep our blood in motion. The Finns and the Laps did not seem to approve of us, and treated us with surly indifference when we asked for boiling water. We stopped for a whole day at Vologda, where peasants sold us hand-made lace, and at Petrozavodsk, and then journeyed fairly steadily up to Kandalaksha, where we met a number of our own Tommies and Marines. They greeted us with cheers, and some of them came and had tea and sang to us.

Two days later we had to disembark at midnight, as a bridge was broken and our train could not pass. Heavily laden with suit-cases, we staggered up hill and down dale, tobogganing on cabin trunks when we came to a slope.

Mamasha, who had sprained her ankle earlier in the week

by dancing a jig to warm her frozen feet, hobbled in the rear, supported on either side by two of her adopted daughters. It was difficult to get her across the ice, and she stood at the edge pathetically waving a crutch, which she had borrowed from a wounded Belgian, and singing in a mournful key, "Oh, why did I leave my little back room in Blooms-bur-ee?"

"Why did we leave Moscow?" I groaned, thinking of the warm room in the hotel, "to come on this wild jaunt."

A tall blue-clad French officer came to our rescue. He was a great friend of ours, and we had nicknamed him "Prince Charming," because he was always so intensely wide awake when every one else was sleepy. When I was bored I used to seek him out and quarrel with him. He responded beautifully. At the moment he was still suffering from the severe defeat in an argument which we had had earlier in the day. He gave Mamasha his arm and ignored me.

"Moscow," he said, to no one in particular, "is for ze military and not for ze bad leetle girls"; and Mamasha, limping painfully, laughed at me over her shoulder.

CHAPTER XIII
Refugees in Murmansk

THE TRAIN ON the other side of the bridge was composed of fourth-class carriages in an unspeakable condition of dirt and airlessness, without water or sanitary arrangements of any description. It was tenanted by bugs, which we called the "Red Guard" on account of their colour and their frequent attacks in massed formation. They kept us awake, and we wrote verses about them, studies in entomology, the chorus of which ran thus :—

> "At night when we wished to be sleeping
> The little Red Guard came creeping.
> We saw them here and we saw them there,
> We watched them stroll through our neighbour's hair,
> And we dozed to the tune of their cheeping."

Mamasha declared that she had a tame one.

The seats in our carriage were wooden and so crowded that some of us were obliged to remain standing up all night. Before starting we had to collect wood for the stoves and make some attempt to sweep out the carriage. The latter we abandoned after a few minutes, as by cleaning we destroyed the dug-outs of the insects and roused them to a counter-offensive of a particularly irritating nature. We were, by this time, dreadfully tired, but owing to the condition of the wagon and the lack of space we could not sleep, and so sat huddled together, wide-eyed and a little cross, looking out of the window at the grey sky, lonely snow-covered hills, and distant water.

IN THE STORM

The Land of the Midnight Sun has a romantic title, but a desolate appearance. We passed through Kola and travelled steadily till we reached Murmansk the following midnight. We had, of course, expected a little town something like Archangel and were utterly taken aback at what we saw. Miles of desolate land stretched before us. Hills with bare trees surrounded the port. At intervals wooden huts were scattered, and higher up we saw what appeared to be long cattle-sheds, but which we afterwards learned to call the "baraks," houses divided into cubicles where refugees, waiting for the boat, were living. Several trains, which appeared to be tenanted all the year round, were standing on the lines, and the ground was covered with snow. There were no shops of any kind, and far up on the hill we saw a tiny graveyard filled with unpainted wooden crosses.

After passports and particulars had been collected we were housed in the train for four days; then some moved to the "Wagon-Lit," others to the "Consulate," and to the remainder Barak No. 25 was allotted. The latter almost defies description. It was a low wooden building, with double windows tightly sealed and made so as not to open. There was a door on either side, and two stoves in the middle, where no light penetrated. The shed, which was arranged to hold a hundred and sixty people, was built like a church with three aisles, divided on each side into small horse-boxes, roofed in such a way that, at a pinch, people could sleep above as well as inside them. Each horse-box was provided with a shelf and two planks to be used as beds. They were not wholly divided one from another, so that privacy could only be insured by hanging up rugs or coats.

On our arrival we discovered the place empty, but so appallingly dirty that we could, at first, only clean it with a spade. It had been occupied before us by Russian workmen, who had left old sheepskins and tins, etc., everywhere. The odour was nauseating, and when we found the windows would not open, we threw a saucepan through the one opposite our box and so dislodged a pane and kept a permanent supply of fresh air. Insects here were even more abundant than in the train, but fortunately we had plenty of Keating's powder, and, by dint of washing three times a day in a solution of corrosive sublimate, we managed to keep clean. On the first day we had a little difficulty, as the tovarishchi returned and wanted to oust us. Afterwards, when they found that we did not wish to move, they suggested occupying the middle aisle while we kept to the side ones. We, knowing the ways of the tovarishchi, were unwilling, and matters looked very unpleasant until the authorities came to some amicable arrangement and we were left in peace.

For four days we lived quietly, scrubbing, scouring, cooking, chopping our own wood and drawing our own water, and then quite unexpectedly we were invaded by a train-load of two hundred and seven French and Belgian working-class people. We had them above us, behind us, and on either side of us. They spent their time in doing the family washing, filling the aisles with flapping wet linen, scolding screaming children, trying to shut our window, over which we mounted guard, and hammering, hammering all day and nearly all night. They rarely seemed to clean out their cubicles, and certainly they never took the children for walks. It was of course difficult to exercise, as there was only one good road. The rest of the ground was underbrush and bog, and so the children either played round the baraks, near the moats where dirty water was poured, or close to the garbage boxes, which, in spite of the cold weather, smelt so unpleasant that we drew shawls over our faces when we passed them.

Of course illness broke out. The window we had smashed was the only means of ventilating the building, which lodged two hundred and fifteen people. The air grew daily more vitiated and an officer, who wanted to come and see us, drew back when he reached the door, saying: "God Lord, it's worse than a gas attack!" Small-pox started, and we were vaccinated one after another with a pen by a doctor who sat on a table, who smoked, and who scorned the use of disinfectants. We had no quinine, and when Spanish influenza declared itself we lay, racked with pain and parched with fever, upon our wooden planks. Some children developed chicken-pox, and an epidemic of measles followed. One little girl had mumps. Two old people died of pleuropneumonia and a child of typhoid, and opposite our window men worked, nailing together the sides of wooden coffins.

Mamasha suffered acutely from malaria, and every day at five o'clock was prostrated with a temperature of a hundred. But she was always smiling, and even when her head was aching with fever she scrubbed floors with disinfectant and helped with the heavy washing, which we had to do ourselves. The family who slept above us were the only people who managed to upset her. This family consisted of five persons: a weary old grandfather, an exceedingly dirty mother who dropped sardine oil on the floor and who cleaned her children's heads just over our box, a father with sores all over his face, an imbecile girl of six, and a baby boy of three, covered with vermin. The small boy, Robert (pronounced Robair) by name, was curiously fascinated by our rugs, and when his parents were not looking sidled up, rubbing his dirty little head against them till we were nearly frantic. We could face Bolsheviks and Anarchists - bombardments left us cold - but lice were more than we could bear.

"Look at him," cried Mamasha as Robert arrived, scratching. I shook some Keating's on to the floor and chanted:—

REFUGEES IN MURMANSK

"Robert, Robert, Now is it fair
When you have very little hair
And we have lots
That gets in knots,
To give us fits
By dropping nits
And other bugs
Upon our rugs ?
You think it nice
To play with lice,
You chase with glee
The sportive flea - "

"Finish it, Mamasha." But Mamasha was beyond verse-making. With the air of a cat stalking a mouse she was stealthily creeping towards the wall, a small piece of tissue paper clasped between the finger and thumb of her outstretched hand. She made a sudden pounce. "Got him!" she cried triumphantly.

Our nights were even more disturbed than our days. All the grown-up people seemed to have coughs, and the children, unused to perpetual daylight and bitten by insects, could not sleep, and cried until early morning.

Sometimes an energetic materfamilias, unable to rest, got up and did the family washing, letting the water drip through the boards which formed her floor and another party's ceiling, thereby causing a quarrel, during which obscene language was freely used and other people, awakened by the noise, uttered shrill rebukes until the whole barak was disturbed. Our bodies ached, and when we did manage to snatch a little sleep we were restless, as lack of nourishing food had made us so thin that lying on planks was painful. We were fed as well as it was possible when all provisions were imported, and the French authorities daily gave out rations of bully-beef, ships' biscuits, sardines, and tea. Tinned milk was supplied to children and invalids.

Bread was scarce, but French biscuits dipped in water made quite a good substitute.

Each barak had a kitchen attached to it, and the women took it in turns to cook hot soup made of beans, bully-beef, and any oddment which could be spared. We waited in queues at twelve o'clock, each holding some sort of a vessel, and the soup was ladled out of large bins. We carried it back to our horse-boxes and supplemented it with sardines or any other tinned food which we happened to have. It was a detestable concoction, but as it was the only hot meal we could have we drank it without complaining. Mamasha and I had tin mugs, in which we ate all manner of food-stuffs, so that our soup acquired after a time a curious flavour.

Fatigue parties were also organized for chopping wood and drawing water, and in this way the fires were kept alight all day and boiling water could be obtained at any time between eight and six. This was a great advantage as we could hang rugs in front of our box and, by lavish use of hot water and carbolic soap, keep fairly clean.

"Is Miss Power here?" I once heard.

Mamasha's apologetic reply followed: "I'm so sorry, she's having a bath."

"Really, is there a bath-room here?"

"Oh, no, but" (proudly) "we have two cups and an earthenware jar."

We soon became lost to all sense of modesty, and I shall never forget the horrified expression of a little Yorkshire man, who had travelled with us and who looked one day into our box as he was shaving and whispered hoarsely: "For Gawd's sake, gurrls, doan't put yer 'eds out; there's a walrus a-washin' of 'isself in the passage" - and we heard the fat French peasant, our neighbour, breathing heavily as he performed his ablutions where there was more room for him to move.

We did not lack entertainments, but we rarely felt well enough to attend them. Concerts were given in the different baraks, moving pictures shown in two sheds which were arranged as cinemas, and on Sunday the American Y.M.C.A. chaplain held an informal church service at the British Consulate, where a curly-headed boy played hymns on the mandoline, asking the preacher, when he could not remember the tune, "Say, sir, do you mind humming that? I've forgotten how it goes."

Peasants and Chinese labourers wandered through the baraks daily, offering extraordinarily large sums of money for second-hand clothing, pots and pans, and crockery.

"We have nothing," they said, "and you go to a country where everything is cheap."

Most of them possessed only the clothes they were wearing, and, as they could not buy anything in Murmansk, were delighted to spend what money they had on garments which were still serviceable though old-fashioned.

Our boat eventually arrived, but remained in harbour for a month, while the carpenters were busy putting up extra berths and hammocks. It was delightfully camouflaged, and we used to go down to the quay and look at it longingly, but only when the British transport office was burnt down were we hustled away by the authorities, who feared trouble. And so, carrying our luggage on stretchers, we waved a glad goodbye to Murmansk. We were a cosmopolitan set - French, Belgians, Serbs, Poles, Russians, and English, and the ship was German, a Portuguese prize with a British crew, chartered by the French Government for Belgian refugees. We were on board seventeen days, sometimes moving, sometimes stationary, two thousand of us in a ship provisioned for eight hundred. Illness, infectious and otherwise, increased daily, and the doctor was distracted by symptoms described in every foreign language but his native English. In the danger zone we were never without our life-belts, and once we heard a depth-charge, which showed that a submarine was at hand.

At last we arrived, so dirty, weary, and infectious, so worn-out with a journey that had covered a period of three months, that we could hardly realize it was summer and we were in England.

"We can disembark! hurrah!" cried Mamasha. She seized her suitcase and rushed upstairs. Suddenly she gripped my arm and stared skywards. I followed her gaze, and we sat down on the deck in despair, for there, floating from the mast, a yellow patch among the white clouds, was the quarantine flag.

www.ingramcontent.com/pod-product-compliance
Lightning Source LLC
Chambersburg PA
CBHW010248010526
44119CB00055B/776